A *Campbell* COOKBOOK

COOKING
WITH
SOUP

608 skillet dishes, casseroles, stews, sauces, gravies, dips, soup mates and garnishes

Table of Contents

DEDICATION

To the millions of American Homemakers who work magic with convenience foods.

Helpful Notes about this Book

Of all the convenience foods that give you a head start to better meals, cans of condensed soup are probably the most versatile.

When you open a can of soup—to use as a soup, or as sauce, or as a cooking ingredient—you have much of the work already done for you.

The special advantages of soups for cooking are that they are:
- Double-rich and double-thick.
- Expertly seasoned as by a chef.
- Extra flavorful.
- Cream soups are creamy smooth every time.

You will find that a casserole is half-ready at the start when soup is the sauce; vegetables are extra-seasoned and enriched. You can toss a savory salad with soup dressing; broil a sandwich with soup topping; serve new cocktail dips that are quick and delicious, with soup as the base. You can even add new character to cakes with condensed soups . . . tomato soup cake recipes have long been treasured by homemakers.

ARRANGEMENT OF THE BOOK

The first half of this book gives you hundreds of recipes for meat dishes, casseroles, vegetables, and sauces—all made with condensed soups. The second half tells how to serve soups in new ways—with added ingredients; as combination soups (soup mates), and with various garnishes.

Each recipe has been carefully tested. To figure condensed soup portions, remember a can contains 1¼ cups soup; this makes 2½ cups when mixed with a can of liquid, or 2 to 3 servings.

Asterisks (*) are used in menus to show items for which there are recipes (check index). All recipes are listed in the index at end of book.

May you enjoy Cooking with Soup.

Carolyn Campbell

Home Economics Department
Campbell Soup Company
Camden, N. J. 08101

Easy Rules for Cooking with Condensed Soups

A can of condensed soup is a constant help in your kitchen—whether you use it for white sauce in a casserole or for cooking liquid in a stew. The cream soups, which are useful in so many recipes, include:

Cream of Celery	Cream of Mushroom
Cream of Chicken	Cream of Vegetable

Often one kind of cream soup may be substituted for another. You will find recipes suggesting this all through the book.

Two other soups with countless uses are:

Cheddar Cheese   Tomato

The following chart gives you some "rules of thumb" to use in creating your own recipes with condensed soups as cooking sauces (see SAUCERY chapter for special sauces with specific directions):

Tomato Souper Sauce   Use condensed tomato soup just as it comes from the can or thin a bit with water, if desired. Season as you like with a little prepared mustard, horseradish, herbs, Worcestershire, etc. Use as pour-on sauce for hamburgers, pork chops, and other meats.

Gravy	Add a can of condensed cream soup or golden mushroom soup to 2 to 3 tablespoons of meat drippings (or butter); stir in ¼ cup water or more as needed for thickness desired.
White Sauce or Cream Sauce	Use canned condensed cream soups or Cheddar cheese soup in almost any recipe that calls for white sauce or cream sauce. Thin with ¼ to ½ cup milk or water for medium white sauce for dishes such as creamed chicken or creamed vegetables. One can makes enough sauce for ½ to 1 cup diced or chopped cooked meat (chicken, turkey, ham, tuna, shrimp, crab) or 4 sliced hard-cooked eggs . . . plus seasonings as desired. One can soup also makes enough pour-on sauce for: 1 pound meat as meat loaf, 1 pound fish fillets, 2 pounds chicken parts, 2 cups cooked vegetables (two 1-pound cans; two 10-ounce packages, frozen), 6 croquettes or chops, 8-egg omelets, 4 to 6 sandwiches.
Casseroles	1 can of any condensed cream soup (or Cheddar cheese or tomato soup) plus ¼ cup water or milk (or more as needed) makes enough sauce for about 2 cups cooked macaroni or noodles (about 4 ounces uncooked) or 1½ cups cooked rice (about ½ cup uncooked). Add seasonings and other ingredients (such as cooked meat or vegetables) as desired.
Meat Stock or Broth	Use canned condensed beef broth or chicken broth or consomme in place of homemade stock. Good for many kinds of stews and pot roasts.
Chicken Stew	Use any of the cream soups, chicken broth, or chicken soups for part of water for cooking. If using a vegetable soup or one with noodles or rice, add towards end of cooking time.
Meat Stew or Pot Roast	Use consomme or beef broth or golden mushroom or tomato soup for part of water or other liquid to cook meat. For vegetables in stew, use one of vegetable soups; add towards end of cooking time since vegetables are already cooked.
Homemade Soup	Add canned condensed soup for extra flavor and body.

Skillet And Top-Stove Dishes

A delicious dish you cook in one pan—and quickly. Who could ask more? No wonder homemakers grow enthusiastic about the flavor, ease, and wonderful versatility of these favorite main dishes.

The basics of skillet cooking are simple. Have a heavy-bottom pan that heats evenly, roomy enough to hold all the ingredients without crowding. (Of course, many of the recipes may be prepared in a chafing dish, large heavy saucepan, or one of the electric utensils.)

Combine foods. As in casseroles, most of these recipes call for meat or fish or cheese—plus a pasta or potatoes—plus sauce. Condensed soups used as sauces give luscious flavor, mingling through all the ingredients and resulting in irresistible eating. See how often the recipes suggest using one soup for another to give a slight flavor variation—as you prefer.

Serve your quick supper dish piping hot, with a crisp salad and warm rolls. Now—collect the compliments.

SEAFOOD MARYLAND

1 can (10 ounces) frozen condensed cream of shrimp soup
½ cup light cream
2 cups cut-up cooked seafood (lobster, shrimp, white fish)
1 tablespoon chopped parsley
1 teaspoon lemon juice
Toast

Heat soup and cream together slowly until soup is thawed; stir often. Add seafood, parsley, and lemon juice. Heat. Serve over toast. 3 to 4 servings.

MACARONI AND CHEESE

¼ cup chopped onion
1 tablespoon butter or margarine
1 can (11 ounces) condensed
  Cheddar cheese soup
½ cup milk
3 cups cooked macaroni

Cook onion in butter until tender. Blend in soup; gradually add milk. Heat; stir often. Mix in macaroni. Heat, stirring. 4 to 6 servings.

BEEF MEXICALI

1 boneless chuck (about 3½ pounds)
2 tablespoons flour
2 tablespoons shortening
1 can (1 pound) tomatoes
½ cup water
1 cup chopped onion
½ cup diced green pepper
2 teaspoons chili powder
1 can (11 ounces) condensed chili
  beef soup
Corn bread

Cut meat into thin strips, trim fat; sprinkle with flour. In skillet, brown meat in shortening; pour off fat. Add remaining ingredients except soup and corn bread. Cover; cook over low heat 1 hour. Stir now and then. Add soup; cook covered ½ hour longer or until tender. Stir now and then. Serve over corn bread. 6 servings.

YUMMY PORCUPINE MEATBALLS

1 can (10¾ ounces) condensed
  tomato soup
1 pound ground beef
1⅓ cups packaged pre-cooked rice
1 egg, slightly beaten
¼ cup finely chopped onion
1 teaspoon salt
1 small clove garlic, minced
2 tablespoons shortening
½ soup can water
1 teaspoon prepared mustard

Mix ¼ cup soup with beef, rice, egg, onion, and salt. Shape into 16 meatballs. Brown meatballs and garlic in shortening; pour off fat. Blend in remaining soup, water, and mustard. Cover; simmer for 20 minutes or until done. Stir now and then. 4 servings.

CHUNKY CHICKEN HASH

1 can (10½ ounces) condensed
    cream of mushroom soup
⅓ to ½ cup milk
1 can (5 ounces) boned chicken or
    turkey, or 1 cup diced cooked
    chicken or turkey
1 can (8 ounces) cut green beans,
    drained
2 tablespoons diced pimiento
Dash nutmeg
Dash pepper
3 cups hot cooked rice

Blend soup and milk; add chicken, beans, pimiento, nutmeg, and pepper. Heat slowly; stir often. Serve over cooked rice. 4 servings.

SOUPER LEFTOVERS

Leftover roast, steak, or chicken,
    chopped (about 1 cup)
Leftover vegetables (about ½ cup)
1 can (10½ ounces) condensed
    cream of celery soup
Milk or water as needed
Crisp toast slices

Combine all ingredients except toast. Heat and serve on toast or in hot patty shells — a tasty way to "make a meal" out of small amounts of meat and vegetables.

VARIATIONS: Substitute cream of vegetable, chicken, mushroom, or tomato soup for cream of celery soup.

HE-MAN SPANISH RICE

1 pound ground beef
½ cup chopped onion
¼ cup chopped green pepper
1 teaspoon salt
⅛ teaspoon chili powder
½ small clove garlic, minced
1 can (10½ ounces) condensed
    tomato soup
1 cup water
1 teaspoon Worcestershire
⅓ cup rice

Cook beef, onion, green pepper, salt, chili powder, and garlic in skillet until beef is browned; stir to separate meat particles. Add remaining ingredients. Cover; cook 30 minutes or until rice is tender; stir often. 3 to 4 servings.

VEAL PARMESAN

1 pound thin veal cutlet
1 egg, beaten
½ cup bread crumbs
2 tablespoons shortening
1 can (10½ ounces) condensed
   tomato soup
½ soup can water
¼ cup minced onion
1 clove garlic, minced
Dash thyme
4 ounces Mozzarella cheese, thinly
   sliced
Grated Parmesan cheese

Dip veal cutlet in egg, then in bread crumbs. Brown in shortening in oven-proof skillet. Add soup, water, onion, garlic, and thyme. Cook over low heat 45 minutes or until tender; stir now and then. Top with Mozzarella cheese; sprinkle with grated Parmesan cheese. Broil until cheese melts. 4 servings.

SKILLET FRANKS 'N NOODLES

1 pound frankfurters, cut in half
   diagonally
½ cup chopped onion
½ teaspoon basil or oregano,
   crushed
2 tablespoons butter or margarine
1 can (10½ ounces) condensed
   cream of celery soup
½ cup milk
½ cup chopped canned tomatoes
2 cups cooked wide noodles
2 tablespoons chopped parsley

In skillet, brown frankfurters and cook onion with basil in butter until tender. Stir in soup, milk, and tomatoes. Add noodles and parsley. Heat; stir now and then. 4 to 5 servings.

CHINESE PORK

1 cup diced cooked pork
½ cup sliced celery
½ cup cooked bean sprouts
½ cup sliced mushrooms
¼ cup sliced green onion
2 tablespoons salad or peanut oil
1 can (10¾ ounces) condensed
   cream of vegetable soup
¼ cup water
2 teaspoons soy sauce
2 cups cut-up spinach
Chow mein noodles

Cook pork, celery, bean sprouts, mushrooms, and green onion in oil until meat is browned and vegetables are just tender. Blend in soup, water, soy sauce, and spinach. Heat; stir now and then. Serve over noodles. 4 servings.

SPAGHETTI SOUTHERN STYLE

2 slices bacon
1 cup diced cooked beef
1 medium green pepper, sliced
1 medium onion, sliced
¼ to ½ teaspoon chili powder
1 clove garlic, minced
1 can (10½ ounces) condensed
   tomato soup
½ soup can water
6 ounces spaghetti, cooked

Cook bacon in skillet until crisp; remove and crumble. In drippings, cook beef, pepper, onion, chili powder, and garlic until vegetables are tender. Add soup, water, and bacon. Cover; cook over low heat 30 minutes. Stir often. Serve over hot spaghetti. 3 to 4 servings.

SPAGHETTI FRANKFURTER SUPPER

½ cup chopped celery
½ cup chopped onion
2 tablespoons shortening
1 pound frankfurters, cut in ½-inch
   slices
1 can (10½ ounces) condensed
   tomato soup
½ cup water
1 teaspoon Worcestershire
6 ounces spaghetti, cooked

Cook celery and onion in shortening until tender. Add frankfurters; cook until lightly browned. Stir in soup, water, and Worcestershire. Cook about 15 minutes to blend flavors; stir often. Serve over hot cooked spaghetti. 3 to 4 servings.

TUNA SHORTCAKE

1 can (10½ ounces) condensed
   cream of celery or mushroom soup
½ cup milk
1 can (7 ounces) tuna, drained
   and flaked
1 cup cooked peas
1 tablespoon chopped pimiento
Hot biscuits or toast

Blend soup and milk; add tuna, peas, and pimiento. Heat; stir often. Serve over biscuits or toast. 4 servings.

SKILLET CHICKEN DELIGHT

2 pounds chicken parts
¼ cup flour
¼ cup butter or margarine
1 can (10½ ounces) condensed
   chicken gumbo soup
½ soup can water
2 tablespoons ketchup

Dust chicken with flour; brown in butter. Stir in soup, water, and ketchup. Cover; simmer 45 minutes or until chicken is tender. Stir often. 4 to 6 servings.

TUNA A LA KING

½ cup sliced celery
2 tablespoons chopped onion
1 tablespoon butter or margarine
1 can (10½ ounces) condensed
  cream of mushroom soup
½ cup milk
1 can (7 ounces) tuna, drained
  and flaked
2 tablespoons chopped pimiento
Chopped parsley
4 slices toast

In saucepan, cook celery and onion in butter until tender. Blend in soup; gradually stir in milk. Add tuna and pimiento. Heat; stir now and then. Garnish with parsley. Serve over toast. 4 servings.

LAST MINUTE SUPPER

1 can (12 ounces) luncheon meat,
  cut in strips
1 medium onion, thinly sliced
2 tablespoons butter or margarine
1 can (10½ ounces) condensed
  cream of mushroom soup
½ cup milk
2 cups cubed cooked potatoes
  (about 4 medium)
2 tablespoons chopped parsley
Dash pepper

Lightly brown meat and onion in butter until onion is tender. Blend in soup and milk. Add remaining ingredients; cook over low heat 10 minutes or until flavors are blended. Stir often. 4 servings.

TUNA BEAN SUPPER DISH

¼ cup minced onion
2 tablespoons butter or margarine
1 can (10½ ounces) condensed
  cream of celery or mushroom soup
½ cup milk
1 can (7 ounces) tuna, drained and
  flaked
2 hard-cooked eggs, sliced
2 tablespoons chopped pimiento
1 pound green beans, cooked and
  drained

Cook onion in butter until soft but not browned; blend in soup, milk, tuna, eggs, and pimiento. Heat; stir often. Arrange hot beans on platter; pour creamed tuna over. 6 servings.

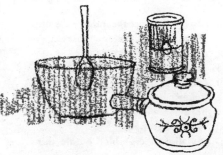

13

Casseroles to Your Credit

Hail to the casserole, favorite way to bring a tasty meal to the table, right in its baking dish.

Choose your own reason for making a casserole tonight. You probably have the ingredients on hand—some meat or fish or poultry—plus a pasta or rice or potatoes to extend them? Add a vegetable for contrast in texture and color.

Now for the perfect sauce that's ready at your fingertips—select a can of soup. It will season and blend together all the other ingredients. The cream soups—cream of vegetable, celery, mushroom, chicken,and Cheddar cheese—go perfectly in almost any combination. Tomato soup also wins honors as a sauce. Often you'll find that one soup can be substituted for another in these recipes. Stir in the soup and your casserole is ready to bake.

Casseroles can be prepared in advance, refrigerated (or often frozen) and baked before serving (allow extra baking time). There's no worry about delay—a casserole waits in a low oven. If the children are to eat ahead, just prepare several smaller baking dishes, or individual servings.

Unexpected company coming? Reach for a can of soup, spaghetti, a can of tuna . . . another good casserole is on the way.

PERFECT TUNA

1 can (10½ ounces) condensed cream of vegetable, celery, chicken, or mushroom soup
⅓ to ½ cup milk
1 can (7 ounces) tuna, drained and flaked
2 hard-cooked eggs, sliced
1 cup cooked peas
1 cup slightly crumbled potato chips

In 1-quart casserole, blend soup and milk; stir in tuna, eggs, and peas. Top with chips. Bake in a 350° oven 30 minutes. 3 to 4 servings.

TOMATO BEEF CASSEROLE

1 medium onion, chopped
1 tablespoon shortening
1 can (10½ ounces) condensed
   tomato soup
½ cup water
1 cup cubed cooked beef
½ cup cooked cut green beans
1 cup cooked noodles
½ cup shredded Cheddar cheese

Lightly brown onion in shortening. Add remaining ingredients except cheese. Pour into a 1-quart casserole. Top with cheese. Bake in a 375° oven 25 minutes or until hot and bubbly. 4 servings.

VARIATION: If desired, ½ pound ground beef can be browned with the onion and substituted for the cooked beef.

YANKEE NOODLE BAKE

8 frankfurters, sliced
¼ cup chopped onion
2 tablespoons butter or margarine
2 cups cooked medium noodles
1 can (10½ ounces) condensed
   tomato soup
½ cup water
1 teaspoon prepared mustard
¼ cup buttered bread crumbs

Brown frankfurters and cook onion in butter until tender. Combine with noodles, soup, water, and mustard in 1½-quart casserole; top with crumbs. Bake in a 350° oven 30 minutes. 4 servings.

CHICKEN PIE

1 can (10½ ounces) condensed
   cream of mushroom soup
½ soup can water
2 tablespoons minced onion
2 tablespoons chopped parsley
Dash leaf thyme, crushed
Dash pepper
1 cup cubed cooked chicken
¾ cup cooked carrot strips
¾ cup diced cooked potato
1 cup packaged biscuit mix
¼ teaspoon dehydrated onion
   flakes
⅛ teaspoon poultry seasoning
⅓ cup milk
2 tablespoons fine dry bread
   crumbs

Blend soup, water, onion, parsley, thyme, and pepper in 1½-quart casserole; add chicken, carrots, and potatoes. Bake in a 450° oven 15 minutes. Meanwhile, combine biscuit mix, onion flakes, poultry seasoning, and milk; roll to fit top of casserole. Place on hot chicken mixture; prick with fork and sprinkle with crumbs. Bake 15 minutes more. 3 to 4 servings.

15

SAVORY SPAGHETTI CASSEROLE

1 pound ground beef
½ cup chopped onion
¼ cup chopped green pepper
2 tablespoons butter or margarine
1 can (10½ ounces) condensed
  cream of mushroom soup
1 can (10½ ounces) condensed
  tomato soup
1 soup can water
1 clove garlic, minced
1 cup shredded sharp process
  cheese
½ pound spaghetti, cooked and
  drained

Cook beef, onion, and green pepper in butter until meat is lightly browned and vegetables are tender; stir to separate meat particles. Add soups, water, and garlic; heat. Blend with ½ cup cheese and cooked spaghetti in a 3-quart casserole; top with remaining cheese. Bake in a 350° oven 30 minutes or until bubbling and hot. 4 to 6 servings.

TURKEY STROGANOFF

¼ cup chopped green pepper
2 tablespoons chopped onion
2 tablespoons butter or margarine
1 can (10½ ounces) condensed
  cream of mushroom soup
½ cup sour cream
¼ cup milk
2 cups cooked noodles
1½ cups diced cooked turkey
½ teaspoon paprika

Cook green pepper and onion in butter until tender. In 1-quart casserole, blend soup, sour cream and milk; stir in remaining ingredients. Bake in a 350° oven 35 minutes. 4 servings.

SEAFOOD POTATO PIE

½ cup sliced celery
2 tablespoons chopped onion
2 tablespoons butter or margarine
1 can (10 ounces) frozen condensed
  cream of shrimp soup
½ cup milk
1 can (6 ounces) shrimp, drained
1 can (6 ounces) lobster, drained
½ cup cooked peas
Dash Angostura bitters
Dash ground thyme
1 cup mashed potatoes (use ¼ cup
  instant mashed potato and prepare as directed on package)
2 tablespoons shredded sharp
  cheese, if desired

Cook celery and onion in butter until tender. Blend in soup, milk, shrimp, lobster, peas, bitters, and thyme. Heat slowly, until soup is thawed; stir often. Pour into 1½-quart casserole. Arrange potatoes around edge of casserole; sprinkle with cheese. Bake in a 450° oven 15 minutes or until potatoes are browned. 4 servings.

16

FIX AHEAD CHICKEN
(pictured on back cover)

2 pounds chicken parts
2 tablespoons shortening
1 can (10½ ounces) condensed
   cream of chicken soup
½ soup can milk
¼ teaspoon poultry seasoning
¼ teaspoon salt
Dash pepper
4 medium carrots, cut lengthwise
   in quarters
6 small onions
1 package (10 ounces) frozen lima
   beans

Brown chicken in shortening; place in a 2-quart casserole. Discard drippings. Stir soup, milk, and seasonings together; heat. Add carrots and onions. Cover; cook over low heat for 10 minutes; stir often. Add lima beans; cook until separated; stir often. Pour over chicken. Cover; immediately refrigerate until 1 hour and 15 minutes before serving. Bake, covered, in a 375° oven for 1 hour. Uncover; bake 15 minutes more or until chicken is tender. If cooked for serving immediately (not refrigerated) decrease baking time of covered casserole 15 minutes. 4 generous servings.

TUNA OR CHICKEN CASSEROLE

1 can (10¾ ounces) condensed
   cream of vegetable soup
½ cup milk
2 cups cooked noodles
1 can (7 ounces) tuna, drained and
   flaked
2 tablespoons diced pimiento
2 tablespoons chopped parsley
2 tablespoons buttered bread
   crumbs

Blend soup and milk. Add noodles, tuna, pimiento, and parsley. Pour into 1½-quart casserole; top with crumbs. Bake in a 350° oven for 30 minutes or until hot and bubbling. 4 servings. VARIATIONS: Substitute 1 can (5 ounces) boned chicken for tuna. Use Cheddar cheese, cream of celery, mushroom, or chicken soup in place of cream of vegetable soup.

SPINACH MUSHROOM CASSEROLE

2 packages (10 ounces each) frozen
   spinach, cooked and drained
2 cups cooked noodles
1 cup shredded process cheese
1 can (10½ ounces) condensed
   cream of mushroom soup
⅓ cup milk
⅛ teaspoon ground nutmeg

Arrange layers of spinach, noodles, and ¾ cup cheese in 1½-quart baking dish or casserole. Blend soup with milk and nutmeg; pour over. Top with remaining cheese. Bake in a 375° oven 45 minutes. 4 servings.

FAVORITE HAM 'N POTATO BAKE

1 can (10½ ounces) condensed
  cream of celery, chicken, or
  mushroom soup
½ to ¾ cup milk
Dash pepper
4 cups sliced potatoes
1 cup diced cooked ham
1 small onion, sliced
1 tablespoon butter or margarine
Paprika

Combine soup, milk, and pepper. In buttered 2-quart casserole, arrange layers of potatoes, ham, onion, and soup sauce. (Be sure ham is covered to prevent drying.) Dot top with butter; sprinkle with paprika. Cover. Bake in a 375° oven for 1 hour. Uncover; bake 15 minutes more or until potatoes are done. 4 to 6 servings. VARIATION: Substitute 1 cup diced cooked chicken for ham.

MACARONI AND CHEESE—FAMILY STYLE

½ cup ground or finely chopped
  cooked ham
¼ cup chopped onion
2 tablespoons butter or margarine
1 can (10½ ounces) condensed
  cream of mushroom soup
½ cup milk
1 cup shredded sharp Cheddar
  cheese
2 cups cooked macaroni
2 tablespoons buttered bread
  crumbs

Lightly brown ham and onion in butter. Stir in soup, milk, and ¾ cup cheese. Heat until cheese melts; stir often. Blend sauce with macaroni; pour into buttered 1½-quart casserole. Sprinkle remaining cheese and crumbs on top. Bake in a 350° oven 30 minutes or until nicely browned and bubbling. Makes 4 servings.

OYSTER 'N HAM NOODLE BAKE

½ cup chopped cooked ham
¼ cup chopped onion
2 tablespoons butter or margarine
1 can (10 ounces) frozen condensed
   oyster stew
Dash "Tabasco" sauce
½ cup milk
2 tablespoons flour
1½ cups cooked green noodles
Grated Parmesan cheese

Brown ham and cook onion in butter until onion is tender. Add oyster stew and "Tabasco" sauce. Heat until thawed. Make smooth paste of milk and flour. Pour into soup mixture; simmer 3 to 4 minutes; stir constantly until thick and smooth. (Do not boil.) Combine sauce and hot noodles in 1-quart casserole; sprinkle cheese on top. Place under broiler for 5 minutes or until browned on top. 2 to 3 servings.

PORK CHOP-BEAN BAKE

6 pork chops, trimmed
1 can (10½ ounces) condensed
   cream of celery or mushroom soup
Dash leaf thyme or dill seed
2 packages (9 ounces each) frozen
   cut green beans, thawed (or two
   1-pound cans cut green beans,
   drained)
¼ teaspoon salt
⅛ teaspoon pepper

In oven-proof skillet, brown chops on both sides. Remove from pan; pour off drippings. Blend in soup and thyme; stir in beans. Arrange chops on top; sprinkle with salt and pepper. Cover; bake in a 350° oven 45 minutes or until chops are tender. Uncover; cook to desired consistency, 5 to 10 minutes. 6 servings.

BUBBLING FISH BAKE

¼ cup chopped onion
2 tablespoons butter or margarine
1 can (10½ ounces) condensed
   cream of vegetable, celery, or
   mushroom soup
½ cup milk
1 cup shredded sharp Cheddar
   cheese
2 cups cooked macaroni or noodles
1 can (8 ounces) salmon, or 1 can
   (7 ounces) tuna, drained and
   flaked
2 tablespoons buttered bread
   crumbs

Cook onion in butter until tender. Stir in soup, milk, ¾ cup cheese, macaroni, and fish. Pour into a 1½-quart casserole. Top with bread crumbs and remaining cheese. Bake in a 350° oven 30 minutes or until lightly browned and bubbling. 4 servings.

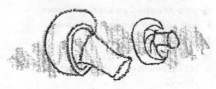

CHICK 'N HAM BAKE

1 can (4 ounces) sliced mushrooms, drained
2 tablespoons chopped onion
2 tablespoons chopped green pepper
1 small clove garlic, minced
Dash leaf thyme
2 tablespoons butter or margarine
1 can (10½ ounces) condensed cream of chicken soup
2 cups cooked spaghetti
1½ cups diced cooked ham
1 cup cooked tomatoes

Cook mushrooms, onion, green pepper, garlic, and thyme in butter until tender. Combine with remaining ingredients; pour into buttered 1½-quart casserole. Bake in a 350° oven 30 minutes. 4 servings.

OVEN MACARONI

¼ cup chopped onion
1 tablespoon butter or margarine
1 can (11 ounces) condensed Cheddar cheese soup
½ cup milk
2 cups cooked macaroni
2 tablespoons buttered bread crumbs

Cook onion in butter until tender. Blend in soup; gradually stir in milk. In buttered 1-quart casserole, combine sauce and cooked macaroni. Sprinkle crumbs on top. Bake in a 375° oven about 30 minutes or until browned and bubbling. 4 servings.

PINWHEEL CASSEROLE

1½ cups cubed cooked beef, lamb, pork, or veal
¼ teaspoon oregano, crushed
2 tablespoons butter or margarine
1 can (10½ ounces) condensed golden mushroom soup
¼ cup water
½ cup chopped canned tomatoes
1 cup cooked cut green beans
1 cup biscuit mix
⅓ cup milk
2 tablespoons grated Parmesan cheese

In saucepan, brown meat with oregano in butter. Stir in soup, water, tomatoes, and green beans. Pour into 1½-quart casserole. Bake at 450°F. for 10 minutes. Meanwhile, combine biscuit mix and milk; mix as directed on package. Roll out into 8-inch square; sprinkle with cheese. Roll up jelly roll fashion; cut into 8 slices. Place biscuits around edge. Bake 15 minutes more or until browned. 4 servings.

SHRIMP 'N SHELL CASSEROLE

1 can (10 ounces) frozen condensed
  cream of shrimp soup
1 cup milk
¼ cup sherry (optional)
2 tablespoons chopped parsley
1 teaspoon curry powder
1 pound shrimp, cooked, cleaned,
  and sliced
2 cups cooked shell macaroni

Combine soup, milk, sherry, parsley, and curry powder. Heat until soup is thawed; stir often. In 1-quart casserole, blend sauce, shrimp, and macaroni. Bake in a 375° oven 25 minutes. 4 servings.

FRANK-POTATO PIE

1 can (10½ ounces) condensed
  cream of celery soup
¾ cup milk
¼ cup finely chopped onion
2 to 3 teaspoons prepared mustard
4 cups diced cooked potatoes
  (about 4 medium)
½ pound frankfurters, slit
  lengthwise

Combine soup, milk, onion, and mustard. In buttered 1½-quart casserole, arrange alternate layers of potatoes, sauce, and frankfurters. Cover; bake in a 400° oven 30 minutes. 4 servings.

SEAFOOD BAKE

1 can (10½ ounces) condensed
  cream of mushroom soup
⅓ cup salad dressing
⅓ cup milk
1 can (6 ounces) shrimp, drained
1 can (7 ounces) tuna or 1 can
  (7 ounces) crab, drained and
  flaked
1 can (5 ounces) water chestnuts,
  drained and sliced
1 cup finely diced celery
2 tablespoons chopped parsley
2 teaspoons grated onion
2 cups cooked macaroni
Paprika

In 1½-quart casserole, blend soup, salad dressing, and milk. Mix in all other ingredients except paprika (sprinkle it on top). Bake in a 350° oven 30 minutes or until hot. 4 to 6 servings.

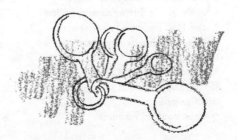

Meat Dishes Make the Meal

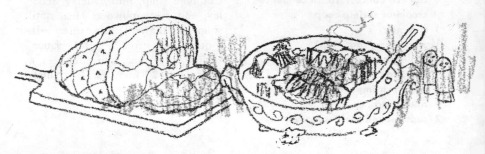

BEEF SPECIALTIES

Meat generally takes the largest part of the family food budget, and often makes the most important part of the meal. The smart homemaker can save time and put new flavor appeal into meat dishes, using canned condensed soups for cooking sauces. You will find new variety for family dinners in these easy, hearty beef dishes. Each has make-this-again flavor.

STEW 'N DUMPLINGS

Carrots or green beans

1 can (8 ounces) whole onions, drained
1 tablespoon butter or margarine
1 can (10¾ ounces) condensed vegetable soup
½ cup water
1½ cups diced cooked beef
1 cup prepared biscuit mix
⅓ cup milk

In saucepan, brown onions in butter. Add soup, water, and meat; heat. Meanwhile, combine biscuit mix and milk; drop by spoonfuls on hot stew making 8 dumplings. Cook uncovered 10 minutes and 10 minutes covered. 4 servings.

CREAMED COOKED BEEF

2 tablespoons chopped onion
1 tablespoon butter or margarine
1 can (10½ ounces) condensed cream of mushroom soup
½ cup water
1 cup diced cooked beef
½ cup cooked peas
Dash pepper
2 cups cooked noodles

Cook onion in butter until tender. Blend in soup and water; add beef, peas, and pepper. Heat; stir often. Serve over noodles. 4 servings.

22

SAUCY BEEF HASH

1 can (10½ ounces) condensed
  cream of celery soup
½ cup chopped parsley
¼ cup minced onion
1½ teaspoons Worcestershire
Dash pepper
2 cups diced cooked beef
2 cups diced cooked potatoes
2 tablespoons shortening
2 tablespoons milk

parsley

Combine ½ can soup, parsley, onion, 1 teaspoon Worcestershire, and pepper. Stir in beef and potatoes. In heavy skillet, cook hash mixture in shortening over medium heat until browned. Meanwhile, combine remaining soup and Worcestershire with milk; heat and serve over hash. 4 servings.

SWISS STEAK WITH VEGETABLES

¼ cup flour
Dash pepper
1 pound round steak (½-inch thick)
2 tablespoons shortening
1 can (10½ ounces) condensed
  onion soup
½ cup water
4 medium carrots, cut in 2-inch
  pieces
4 medium potatoes, cut in half
1 tablespoon chopped parsley

Pound flour and pepper into steak with meat hammer or edge of heavy saucer. Cut into 4 serving pieces. In large skillet, brown steak on both sides in shortening. Add soup, water, carrots, and potatoes. Cover; cook over low heat 45 minutes or until meat and vegetables are tender. Stir now and then. Sprinkle with parsley just before serving. 4 servings.

YANKEE POT ROAST

3 to 4-pound beef pot roast
1 can (10½ ounces) condensed
  onion soup
¼ cup water
2 to 4 tablespoons flour

Brown meat well on all sides in heavy kettle; add soup. Cover; cook over low heat until meat is done—about 2½ to 3 hours. Remove meat; thicken gravy as desired, using a smooth paste made by blending water with flour. About 6 to 8 servings. (If desired, add vegetables —carrots, potatoes, turnips, etc— after meat has been cooking for 2 hours. Season. Cover; cook until vegetables are done—about 1 hour. Remove meat and vegetables to platter; thicken gravy according to directions.)

BARBECUED STEAK SUPREME

2 pounds steak (round or flank, ¾-inch thick)
2 tablespoons seasoned flour
2 tablespoons shortening
⅓ cup minced onion
⅓ cup minced celery
½ clove garlic, minced
1 can (10½ ounces) condensed tomato soup
2 tablespoons brown sugar
2 tablespoons Worcestershire
2 tablespoons lemon juice
2 teaspoons prepared mustard
Dash "Tabasco" sauce

Pound flour into steak. Brown in shortening in a heavy saucepan or skillet, along with onion, celery, and garlic. Add remaining ingredients; stir well; cover. Cook in a 350° oven or on top of range for about 1½ hours or until tender. NOTE: Double all sauce ingredients for additional barbecue sauce to serve over fluffy rice or mashed potatoes. 6 servings.

SOUPER STROGANOFF

1½ pounds round steak, cut in thin strips
¼ cup flour
Dash pepper
¼ cup butter or margarine
1 can (4 ounces) sliced mushrooms, drained
½ cup chopped onion
1 small clove garlic, minced
1 can (10½ ounces) condensed consomme
1 cup sour cream
3 cups cooked noodles

Dust meat with flour and pepper. In skillet, brown meat in butter. Add mushrooms, onion, and garlic; brown lightly. Stir in soup. Cover; cook 1 hour or until meat is tender; stir often. Gradually blend in sour cream; cook over low heat for 5 minutes. Serve over noodles. 4 generous servings.

SMOTHERED STEAK ROLL-UPS

1½ pounds thinly sliced round steak (¼-inch thick)
1½ cups prepared packaged herb-seasoned stuffing
2 tablespoons shortening
1 can (10½ ounces) condensed consomme, cream of vegetable, mushroom, or golden mushroom soup
½ cup water

Cut steak into 6 pieces (about 8x 4"). Pound with meat hammer or edge of heavy saucer. Place ¼ cup stuffing near center of each piece of meat. Roll up; tuck in ends and fasten with skewers or toothpicks. In skillet, brown roll-ups in shortening; pour off fat. Add soup and water. Cover; cook over low heat 1¼ hours or until tender. Stir now and then. 6 servings.

TOMATO BEEF STEW

1 pound beef cubes
2 tablespoons seasoned flour
2 tablespoons shortening
1 can (10½ ounces) condensed
    tomato soup
1 soup can water
6 small whole white onions
6 small carrots, cut in half
3 potatoes, quartered
¼ teaspoon whole thyme

Dust meat with flour; brown in shortening in large heavy pan. Add soup and water. Cover; simmer 1½ hours. Add remaining ingredients. Cover; cook 1 hour or until vegetables are tender. Stir now and then. To thicken, uncover; cook until desired consistency. 4 servings.

EASY SWISS STEAK

1½ pounds round steak (¾-inch
    thick)
2 tablespoons shortening
1 can (10½ ounces) condensed
    golden mushroom soup
½ cup chopped canned tomatoes
¼ cup chopped onion
Dash pepper

Pound steak with meat hammer or edge of heavy saucer. In skillet, brown steak in shortening; pour off fat. Add remaining ingredients. Cover; cook over low heat 1½ hours or until tender. Stir now and then. 4 to 6 servings.

SAUCY BEEF ON ROLLS

2 tablespoons butter or margarine
1½ teaspoons chili powder
1 clove garlic, minced
1 pound thinly sliced round steak
½ cup chopped celery
½ cup chopped onion
1 can (10½ ounces) condensed
    tomato soup
¼ cup water
1 teaspoon vinegar
½ teaspoon salt
6 rolls, toasted and buttered

Melt butter; blend in chili powder and garlic. Add meat; brown lightly; push to one side. Add celery and onion; cook until tender. Stir in soup, water, vinegar, and salt. Cover; cook over low heat for 10 minutes. Uncover; cook an additional 10 minutes. Stir now and then. Serve on rolls. 6 servings.

CARNE QUISADA

¼ cup diced salt pork
2 pounds beef cubes
1 teaspoon paprika
1 can (10½ ounces) condensed
   tomato soup
2 cups water
1 medium green pepper, chopped
1 medium onion, chopped
2 bay leaves
Dash red pepper
2 pounds potatoes, peeled and
   quartered
1 teaspoon salt
10 pitted green olives
1 tablespoon capers, if desired

Partially cook salt pork. Add beef and paprika; brown. Add soup, water, green pepper, onion, bay leaves, and red pepper. Cover; cook over low heat about 2 hours. Add potatoes, salt, olives, and capers; cook 40 minutes longer or until potatoes are tender. Stir now and then. 8 servings.

STEAK IN SAUCE

¼ cup seasoned flour
1½ pounds round steak (about ¾-
   inch thick)
2 tablespoons shortening
1 can (10½ ounces) condensed
   cream of mushroom soup
½ soup can water
½ cup sour cream, if desired

Pound seasoned flour into steak with meat hammer or edge of heavy saucer. In large skillet, brown steak on both sides in shortening. Add soup and water. Cover; cook over low heat 45 minutes or until steak is tender. Stir often. Just before serving stir in sour cream. 4 to 6 servings.

SPICY SHORT RIBS

3 pounds short ribs of beef
¼ cup flour
2 tablespoons shortening
1 can (10½ ounces) condensed
   beef broth
1 cup dried apricots
2 tablespoons brown sugar
2 tablespoons vinegar
¼ teaspoon ground cinnamon
¼ teaspoon ground cloves
¼ teaspoon ground allspice

Dust ribs with flour; brown in shortening in large heavy pan. Pour off excess drippings. Combine remaining ingredients; pour over ribs. Cover; cook over low heat 2½ hours or until ribs are tender; turn ribs and baste with sauce often. 4 to 6 servings.

STROGANOFF STEW

1 boneless chuck (about 3½ pounds)
2 tablespoons shortening
2 cans (10½ ounces each) condensed
   cream of mushroom soup
½ cup sour cream
½ cup water
1 teaspoon paprika
Generous dash pepper
1 pound carrots, halved
1 pound whole small white onions
Cooked wide noodles

Trim fat from meat and cut into 1-inch cubes. In large heavy pan, brown beef in shortening; pour off fat. Add soup, sour cream, water, paprika, and pepper. Cover; cook over low heat 1 hour. Stir now and then. Add vegetables. Cover; cook over low heat 1 hour longer or until meat and vegetables are tender. Stir now and then. Serve with noodles. 6 servings.

CORNED BEEF 'N CABBAGE CASSEROLE

1 can (10½ ounces) condensed
   cream of celery soup
½ cup chopped onion
1 teaspoon dry mustard
1 cup diced cooked corned beef
4 cups coarsely shredded cabbage

Mix all ingredients in 1½-quart casserole. Cover; bake in a 375° oven 45 minutes. 4 servings.

PEPPER STEAK

¼ cup seasoned flour
1½ pounds round steak (about ¾-inch thick)
2 tablespoons shortening
1 can (10½ ounces) condensed
   tomato soup
½ cup water
1 large green pepper, cut into 8
   strips
1 medium onion, sliced
1 clove garlic, minced
1 tablespoon lemon juice
4 thin slices lemon

Pound seasoned flour into steak with meat hammer or edge of heavy saucer. Brown steak on both sides in shortening. Add remaining ingredients. Cover; cook over low heat 45 minutes or until steak is tender; stir often. 4 to 6 servings.

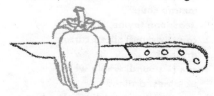

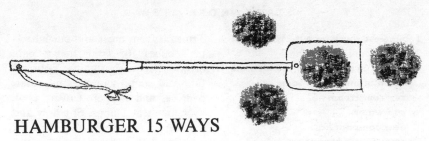

HAMBURGER 15 WAYS

Ground beef makes economy meals with good flavor the whole family enjoys—especially when the meat is seasoned with the addition of soup. Soup prevents shrinkage in meat loaves and burgers; stretches food values while it adds good taste.

SPREAD-A-BURGERS

1½ pounds ground beef
1 can (10½ ounces) condensed tomato or cream of mushroom soup
⅓ cup finely chopped onion
1 tablespoon prepared mustard
1 tablespoon Worcestershire
1 teaspoon prepared horseradish
1 teaspoon salt
Dash pepper
6 frankfurter buns, split and toasted

Thoroughly mix beef, soup, onion, and seasonings. Spread mixture evenly over bun halves; *cover edges completely*. Broil about 4 inches from heat for 12 to 15 minutes. 6 open-face sandwiches.

MEATBALL STEW

1½ pounds ground beef
1 egg, slightly beaten
1 cup small bread cubes
¼ cup finely chopped onion
1 teaspoon salt
2 tablespoons shortening
1 can (10½ ounces) condensed beef broth
1 can (10¾ ounces) condensed tomato soup
¼ teaspoon thyme, crushed
1 can (1 pound) sliced carrots, drained
1 can (1 pound) whole white potatoes, drained
1 can (8 ounces) small whole white onions, drained

Mix beef, egg, bread, onion, and salt; shape into 24 meatballs. Brown in shortening in skillet; pour off fat. Add remaining ingredients. Cook over low heat 20 min.; stir now and then. Top with chopped parsley. 6 servings.

OLD-FASHIONED MEAT LOAF

1 can (10½ ounces) condensed cream of celery or mushroom; or chicken gumbo, tomato, or vegetable soup
2 pounds ground beef
½ cup fine dry bread crumbs
½ cup chopped onion
2 tablespoons chopped parsley
1 tablespoon Worcestershire
1 egg, slightly beaten
1 teaspoon salt
Dash pepper

Combine all ingredients; mix *thoroughly*. Shape *firmly* into a loaf; place in shallow baking pan. (*Thorough* mixing and *firm* shaping will produce a moist, easy-to-slice loaf.) Bake in a 350° oven 1¼ hours. 8 servings. If desired, after loaf has baked 1 hour, garnish top with 4 tomato slices and ½ cup shredded mild cheese; bake 15 minutes more.

TOP-STOVE MEAT LOAF

1½ pounds ground beef
½ cup dry bread crumbs
1 can (10¾ ounces) condensed tomato soup
¼ cup finely chopped onion
1 egg, slightly beaten
1 teaspoon salt
Generous dash pepper
1 tablespoon shortening
¼ cup water
½ teaspoon prepared mustard
2 slices process cheese, cut in half

Thoroughly mix beef, crumbs, ¼ cup soup, onion, egg, and seasonings. Shape *firmly* into 2 loaves; brown on both sides in skillet in shortening. Cover; cook over low heat 25 minutes. Spoon off fat. Stir in remaining soup, water, mustard. Top loaves with cheese. Uncover; cook 10 minutes. 4 to 6 servings.
Oven Method: Mix and shape as above. Bake at 350°F. for 40 minutes. Spoon off fat. Pour remaining soup (omit water) mixed with mustard on loaves; top with cheese. Bake 5 minutes more.

SPAGHETTI WITH MEAT SAUCE

1 pound ground beef
1 to 2 cloves garlic, minced
1 cup chopped onion
2 tablespoons salad oil
2 cans (10½ ounces each) condensed tomato soup
½ soup can water
1 teaspoon salt
1 bay leaf
⅛ teaspoon pepper
⅛ teaspoon leaf thyme
12 ounces thin spaghetti, cooked

Brown beef, garlic, and onion in oil. Blend in soup, water, and seasonings. Simmer 30 minutes; stir often. Serve sauce over spaghetti; sprinkle with grated Parmesan cheese. 6 servings.

SOUPER BURGERS

1 pound ground beef
1 cup chopped celery
1 tablespoon shortening
1 can (10½ ounces) condensed
  onion soup
½ cup water
¼ cup ketchup
1 teaspoon Worcestershire
1 teaspoon prepared mustard
Dash pepper
6 buns, toasted and buttered

Brown beef with celery in shortening; stir to separate meat particles. Add soup, water, and seasonings. Simmer 10 to 15 minutes or until slightly thickened. Stir now and then. Serve on buns. 6 servings.

HAMBURGERS ITALIANO

1 pound ground beef
½ teaspoon salt
Dash pepper
1 can (2 ounces) sliced mushrooms,
  drained
1 small onion, sliced
⅛ teaspoon leaf oregano, crushed
1 small clove garlic, minced
2 tablespoons butter or margarine
1 can (10½ ounces) condensed
  tomato soup
¼ cup water

Combine beef, salt, and pepper; shape into 4 hamburgers. Brown hamburgers along with mushrooms, onion, oregano, and garlic in butter. Stir in soup and water. Cover; cook over low heat 15 minutes; stir often. 4 servings.

MEAT-SHELL PIE

1 can (10¾ ounces) condensed
  tomato soup
1½ pounds ground beef
1 teaspoon salt
1½ teaspoons chili powder
6 frankfurters, split
½ cup chopped onion
2 tablespoons butter or margarine
½ cup shredded process cheese
Grated Parmesan cheese

Place a double layer of foil on cookie sheet. Mix thoroughly ⅓ cup soup, beef, salt, and 1 teaspoon chili powder; pat out firmly into 11-inch circle about ½-inch thick on foil. Turn up edges of foil to catch fat. Firmly press frankfurters, cut side up, into meat in spoke fashion. In saucepan, cook onion with remaining chili in butter until tender; stir in remaining soup; spread over meat. Bake at 450°F. for 15 minutes. Spoon off fat. Sprinkle with cheeses; bake until melted. 6 servings.

MANY WAY MEATBALLS

1 pound ground beef
¼ cup dry bread crumbs
¼ cup minced onion
1 egg, slightly beaten
¼ teaspoon salt
1 can (10½ ounces) condensed Cheddar cheese, cream of celery or mushroom soup
½ cup water
2 tablespoons chopped parsley

Mix beef, bread crumbs, onion, egg, and salt; shape into 16 meatballs. In skillet, brown meatballs; pour off drippings. Stir in soup, water, and parsley. Cover; cook over low heat 20 minutes; stir often. 4 servings.

STUFFED CABBAGE ROLLS

8 large cabbage leaves
1 pound ground beef
1 cup cooked rice
¼ cup chopped onion
1 egg, slightly beaten
1 teaspoon salt
¼ teaspoon pepper
1 can (10½ ounces) condensed tomato soup

Cook cabbage leaves in boiling salted water a few minutes to soften; drain. Combine beef, rice, onion, egg, salt, and pepper with 2 tablespoons soup. Divide meat mixture among cabbage leaves; roll and secure with toothpicks or string. Place cabbage rolls in skillet; pour remaining soup over. Cover; cook over low heat about 40 minutes. Stir often, spooning sauce over rolls. 4 servings.

SOUPER SAUCY MEAT LOAF

1 can (10½ ounces) condensed cream of vegetable or mushroom or tomato soup
¼ cup water
1 cup small bread cubes
¼ cup minced onion
2 tablespoons finely chopped parsley
1 egg, slightly beaten
1 teaspoon salt
⅛ teaspoon pepper
1½ pounds ground beef

Blend soup and water. Combine ½ cup soup mixture with bread, onion, parsley, egg, salt, and pepper; mix *thoroughly* with meat. Shape *firmly* into loaf; place in shallow baking pan (12 x 8 x 2"). Bake in a 350° oven 1 hour 15 minutes. Blend remaining soup with 2 tablespoons drippings. Heat; stir now and then. Serve over loaf. 4 to 6 servings.

NOTE: Garnish loaf made with cream of mushroom soup by sprinkling chopped parsley over the top.

ROLL-IN-ONE MEAT LOAF

1 can (10¾ oz.) condensed tomato
   soup
1½ pounds ground beef
½ cup fine dry bread crumbs
¼ cup minced onion
2 tablespoons chopped parsley
1 egg, slightly beaten
1 teaspoon salt
Dash pepper
1 package (9 ounces) frozen cut
   green beans, cooked, well drained

Combine ½ cup soup with all ingredients except beans. Mix well. On waxed paper, pat into a 12x9-inch shape. Spread beans to within 1 inch of all edges; pat into meat. With aid of waxed paper, roll meat tightly, jelly-roll fashion, starting at long edge. Seal ends; use waxed paper to transfer to baking dish. Bake at 350°F. for 40 minutes. Spoon off fat. Pour remaining soup over loaf. Bake 10 minutes longer. 6 servings.

SWEDISH MEATBALLS

1 pound ground beef
¼ cup fine dry bread crumbs
¼ cup minced onion
1 egg, slightly beaten
2 tablespoons chopped parsley
1 can (10½ ounces) condensed cream
   of celery soup
½ soup can water
1 to 2 tablespoons minced dill pickle
Cooked rice

Mix beef, bread crumbs, onion, egg, and parsley; shape into 24 meatballs. In skillet, brown meatballs; pour off drippings. Stir in soup, water, and pickle. Cover; cook over low heat 20 minutes; stir often. Serve with rice. 4 servings.

STUFFED PEPPERS

4 medium green peppers
½ pound ground beef
½ cup chopped onion
1 tablespoon butter or margarine
1 can (10½ ounces) condensed
   tomato soup
2 cups cooked rice
1 teaspoon Worcestershire
½ teaspoon salt
Dash pepper

Remove tops and seeds from peppers; cook in boiling salted water about 5 minutes; drain. Brown beef and cook onion in butter until tender; stir in ½ can soup and remaining ingredients. Spoon meat mixture into peppers; place in 1½-quart casserole. Bake in a 375° oven 30 minutes. Heat remaining soup and serve over peppers. 4 servings.

Green Bean Casserole   Pages 71 and 106
Old-Fashioned Meat Loaf   Page 29
Scallops Parisienne   Page 93

1 pound ground beef
¼ cup chopped onion
¼ cup chopped green pepper
1 can (10¾ ounces) condensed
   vegetable soup
¼ teaspoon salt
Dash thyme, if desired
Seasoned mashed potatoes (about
   1 cup)

Brown beef and cook onion and green pepper until tender; stir in soup, salt, and thyme. Spoon into 1-quart casserole; place potatoes in mounds around edge of casserole. Bake in a 425° oven 15 minutes. 4 servings.

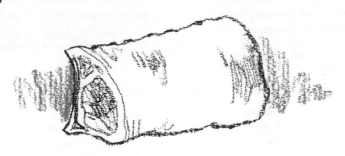

PORK TO PERFECTION

Do you make the most of the good pork values often available in the markets? Condensed soups add new color and flavor to thrifty pork dishes, rich in proteins and B-vitamins. Here are some recipes to help you make varied new main dishes of ham and pork.

BARBECUED LOIN OF PORK

3- to 5-pound loin (or shoulder) of
   pork
1 can (10½ ounces) condensed
   tomato soup
⅓ cup chopped onion
⅓ cup chopped celery
1 clove garlic, minced
2 tablespoons brown sugar
2 tablespoons Worcestershire
2 tablespoons lemon juice or
   vinegar
2 teaspoons prepared mustard
4 drops "Tabasco" sauce

Roast pork in shallow pan at 325° about 45 minutes per pound. One hour before meat is done, pour off drippings. Combine soup and remaining ingredients to make sauce. Pour over meat; continue roasting; spoon sauce over meat often.

Tomato Soup Cake   Page 86
Green Salad with Tomato
French Dressing   Page 81
Mock Sukiyaki   Page 97

GLAZED FRUITED PORK CHOPS

4 pork chops (about 1 pound)
4 slices apple
4 slices orange
Dash ground cinnamon
Dash ground cloves
1 can (10½ ounces) condensed
beef broth
1 tablespoon brown sugar
2 tablespoons orange juice
1 tablespoon cornstarch

Brown chops on both sides; pour off drippings. Place an apple and orange slice on each chop; sprinkle with cinnamon and cloves. Add soup and sugar. Cover; cook over low heat 35 minutes. Mix orange juice and cornstarch until smooth; gradually blend into soup. Cook; stir constantly until slightly thickened; simmer a few minutes or until chops are tender. 4 servings.

HAM BAKE

1 cup diced cooked ham
2 tablespoons chopped onion
⅛ teaspoon tarragon
2 tablespoons butter or margarine
1 can (10½ ounces) condensed
cream of chicken soup
½ cup water
1½ cups cooked noodles
½ cup cooked French style green
beans
2 tablespoons fine dry bread crumbs
½ small clove garlic, minced

Cook ham, onion, and tarragon in 1 tablespoon butter until ham is browned and onion is tender. Stir in soup, water, noodles, and green beans. Pour into buttered 1-quart casserole. Lightly brown crumbs and garlic in remaining tablespoon butter; sprinkle over top of casserole. Bake in a 350° oven 30 minutes or until hot and bubbly. 4 servings.

HURRY-UP PORK HASH

1 medium onion, thinly sliced
2 tablespoons butter or margarine
1 can (10½ ounces) condensed
cream of celery or mushroom soup
½ cup milk
1 teaspoon Worcestershire
1 cup cubed cooked pork
1 cup cubed cooked potatoes
(about 2 medium)
½ cup cooked peas
Dash pepper

Cook onion in butter until lightly browned. Blend in soup, milk, and Worcestershire. Add remaining ingredients. Cook over low heat 10 minutes; stir often. 3 to 4 servings.

GLORI-FRIED CHOPS

4 pork chops (about 1 pound)
1 can (10½ ounces) condensed
cream of vegetable, celery,
mushroom, or tomato soup
¼ to ⅓ cup water

In skillet, brown chops. Pour off fat. Stir in soup, water. Cover; cook over low heat 45 minutes or until tender. Stir now and then. 4 servings.

CREAMY BAKED CHOPS:

Brown chops in oven-proof skillet as above. After adding liquids, cover; bake at 350°F. for 45 minutes or until tender.

PORK CHOPS 'N STUFFING

4 pork chops (about 1 pound)
3 cups soft bread cubes
2 tablespoons chopped onion
¼ cup melted butter or margarine
¼ cup water
¼ teaspoon poultry seasoning
1 can (10½ ounces) condensed
cream of mushroom soup
⅓ cup water

Brown chops on both sides; place in shallow baking dish. Lightly mix together bread cubes, onion, butter, ¼ cup water and poultry seasoning. Place a mound of stuffing on each chop. Blend soup and ⅓ cup water; pour over. Bake in a 350° oven 1 hour or until tender. 4 servings.

PORK CHOP AND POTATO SCALLOP

4 pork chops (about 1 pound)
1 can (10½ ounces) condensed
cream of mushroom soup
½ cup sour cream
¼ cup water
2 tablespoons chopped parsley
4 cups thinly sliced potatoes
Salt
Pepper

Brown chops. Blend soup, sour cream, water, and parsley. In 2-quart casserole, alternate layers of potatoes sprinkled with salt and pepper, and sauce. Top with chops. Cover; bake in a 375° oven 1¼ hours. 4 servings.

LAMB, VEAL, LIVER

Many American housewives repeat their complete range of main dish recipes every two weeks. You can find new mealtime variety and interest in more extensive use of these special meats. Try stewing lamb in savory soup sauce; add zest to veal dishes seasoned quickly and easily with a can of soup. Discover new flavor in nutritious liver simmered in flavorful sauces.

LAMB KABOBS

¼ cup chopped onion
1 clove garlic, minced
1 teaspoon curry powder
⅛ teaspoon ground ginger
2 tablespoons butter or margarine
1 can (10½ ounces) condensed cream of mushroom soup
¼ cup water
1 pound leg of lamb, cut in 1½-inch cubes
2 apples, quartered
1 medium green pepper, cut in 1½-inch pieces
8 small white onions

For sauce, cook onion, garlic, curry powder, and ginger in butter until onion is tender. Add soup and water; cook 5 minutes; stir often. (Partially precook green pepper and white onions if very tender vegetables are desired.) On 4 skewers, alternate lamb, apple, green pepper, and onion; place on broiler rack. Brush kabobs with sauce. Broil, about 4 inches from heat, for 30 minutes or until meat is tender; turn kabobs and brush with sauce every 5 minutes. 4 servings.

MUSHROOM-LAMB CURRY

½ cup chopped onion
½ cup chopped green pepper
½ cup chopped celery
1 large clove garlic, minced
¼ cup butter or margarine
1 pound lamb cubes
2 teaspoons curry powder
1 can (10½ ounces) condensed cream of mushroom soup
1 cup water
3 cups cooked rice

Cook onion, green pepper, celery, and garlic in butter until vegetables are tender; push to side of skillet. Add lamb; brown with curry powder. Blend in soup and water. Cover; cook over low heat 1 hour or until tender; stir often. Serve over rice. 4 servings.

GRANDMOTHER'S LAMB STEW

1 pound lamb cubes
1 large clove garlic, minced
¼ teaspoon leaf thyme, crushed
2 tablespoons butter or margarine
1 can (10½ ounces) condensed
  onion soup
½ soup can water
1 cup diced celery
½ cup cooked tomatoes
½ teaspoon salt
¼ teaspoon pepper
4 medium potatoes (about 1
  pound), quartered
1 package (9 ounces) frozen cut
  green beans

Cook lamb, garlic, and thyme in butter in large heavy pan until lamb is browned. Add soup, water, celery, tomatoes, and seasonings. Cover; cook over low heat about 1 hour. Add potatoes; cover; cook 20 minutes. Add green beans; cover; cook 15 minutes more; stir often. 4 servings.

LAMB RAGOUT

1½ pounds lamb cubes
2 tablespoons flour
¼ cup shortening
1 can (10½ ounces) condensed
  tomato soup
1 soup can water
1 teaspoon salt
⅛ teaspoon pepper
1 clove garlic, minced
⅛ to ¼ teaspoon caraway seed
  (optional)
3 medium potatoes, quartered
  (about 2 cups)
½ medium cabbage, cut in wedges

Dust lamb with flour; brown in shortening in large heavy kettle or pot. Add soup, water, salt, pepper, garlic, and caraway seed. Cover; simmer 1 hour; stir often. Add potatoes to broth; cover and cook 15 minutes. Lay cabbage on top. Cover; cook 30 minutes more or until meat and vegetables are tender. 4 to 6 servings.

VIENNA VEAL AND NOODLES

1½ pounds veal cubes
1 clove garlic, minced
¼ teaspoon marjoram (optional)
2 tablespoons butter or margarine
1 can (10½ ounces) condensed
  cream of mushroom soup
½ soup can water
¼ teaspoon paprika
Cooked noodles

In oven-proof skillet, brown veal, garlic, and marjoram in butter. Blend in soup, water, and paprika. Cover; bake in a 350° oven 1 hour or until tender. Serve with hot noodles. 4 to 6 servings.

VEAL GOULASH

1 pound veal steak (½-inch thick)
2 tablespoons shortening
1 cup sliced mushrooms
¼ cup finely chopped onion
1 can (10½ ounces) condensed
   tomato soup
½ cup sour cream
¼ cup water
1 bay leaf
½ teaspoon salt
¼ teaspoon pepper
1 teaspoon paprika
Cooked rice

Cut veal into 4 pieces. Brown well on both sides in shortening. Add mushrooms and onion; cook until lightly browned. Blend in remaining ingredients except rice. Cover; simmer 45 minutes or until meat is tender; stir often. Remove bay leaf before serving. Serve over rice. 4 servings.

VEAL BIRDS

1 pound thinly sliced veal cutlet
1 cup cooked rice
2 tablespoons butter or margarine
2 tablespoons chopped parsley
2 tablespoons shortening
2 tablespoons chopped onion
1 can (10¾ ounces) condensed
   tomato rice soup
¼ cup water
⅛ teaspoon leaf oregano, if desired

Pound veal with meat hammer; cut into 4 large or 8 small pieces. Combine rice, butter, and parsley; place a small amount on each piece of veal; roll and fasten with toothpicks or skewers. Brown veal birds in shortening along with onion; pour off excess drippings. Combine remaining ingredients; pour over meat. Cover; cook over low heat for 45 minutes. Spoon sauce over meat occasionally. 4 servings. Thin sauce to desired consistency with small amount of water before serving.

SAVORY LIVER SKILLET

1 pound thinly sliced liver, cut in
   strips
2 tablespoons flour
½ medium green pepper, sliced
1 medium onion, sliced
¼ cup shortening
1 can (10½ ounces) condensed
   tomato soup
¼ cup water
1 to 2 thin slices lemon, cut in
   quarters

Dust liver with flour. Brown with green pepper and onion in shortening. Add soup, water, and lemon. Cover; cook over low heat 30 minutes or until liver is tender. Stir often. 4 servings.

LIVER INDIENNE

1 package (8 ounces) frozen chicken
   livers, thawed
½ cup sliced celery
⅓ cup chopped onion
1 teaspoon curry powder
2 tablespoons butter or margarine
1 can (10½ ounces) condensed
   golden mushroom soup
⅓ cup water
Cooked rice

In saucepan, cook livers, celery, onion, and curry in butter until livers are done. Stir in soup and water. Heat; stir now and then. Serve over rice. 2 servings.

CHILI LIVER

4 slices bacon
1 pound liver, sliced
2 tablespoons flour
1 can (10½ ounces) condensed
   onion soup
¼ cup chili sauce or ketchup

Cook bacon until crisp; remove from pan; drain and crumble. Dust liver with flour; brown in bacon drippings. Add bacon and remaining ingredients. Cover; simmer 30 minutes or until tender. Uncover; cook for a few minutes to thicken sauce. 4 servings.

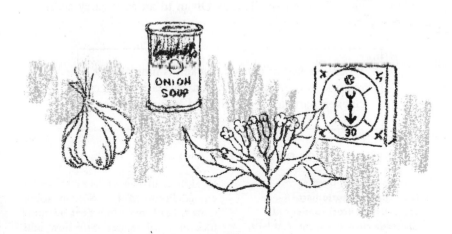

Poultry

There is new versatility to cooking poultry. With chicken parts readily available, either fresh or frozen, and canned chicken handy for hurry-up dinners, chicken comes to the table more often than ever.

You can add to your ways of preparing chicken thanks to flavorful soup sauces. From Glori-fried Chicken to Poulet au Vin here is an international range of quick and easy dishes.

Turkey now comes to the table more often, too. When a large turkey makes its second-act appearance, give it a dramatic switch in flavor and appearance. Choose from Turkey Divan to an easy curry-accented dish, ready in 5 minutes.

> Where cooked or canned chicken is indicated in recipes, turkey may be used instead. Frozen chicken parts are to be thawed before cooking.

GLORI-FRIED CHICKEN

2 pounds chicken parts
2 tablespoons shortening
1 can (10¾ ounces) condensed
   Cheddar cheese, cream of celery,
   chicken, or mushroom soup

In skillet, brown chicken in shortening. Pour off fat. Stir in soup. Cover; cook over low heat 45 minutes or until tender. Stir now and then. Uncover; cook until desired consistency. 4 to 6 servings.

PENTHOUSE CHICKEN

(pictured on cover)

2 pounds chicken parts
¼ cup seasoned flour
Shortening or salad oil
½ medium green pepper, cut in strips
½ cup sliced onion
⅛ to ¼ teaspoon thyme, crushed
1 can (10¾ ounces) condensed tomato soup
¼ cup water
1 teaspoon vinegar

Dust chicken with seasoned flour. Brown in skillet in hot shortening (¼-inch deep). Cover; cook over low heat 45 minutes. Uncover last 10 minutes to crisp. Remove chicken to heated platter; keep warm. Pour off all but 2 tablespoons fat. Add green pepper, onion, and thyme; cook until green pepper is tender. Add remaining ingredients. Heat; stir now and then. Serve over chicken. 4 to 6 servings.

ONE-STEP METHOD:

Omit flour and water. Brown chicken in 2 tablespoons shortening. Pour off fat. Sprinkle with salt, pepper. Add remaining ingredients (increase vinegar to 1 tablespoon). Cover; cook over low heat 45 minutes or until tender. Stir now and then.

DREAMY CHICKEN STEW

1 can (10½ ounces) condensed cream of chicken soup
1½ cups water
1 cup sliced celery
1 medium onion, quartered
1 teaspoon salt
¼ teaspoon poultry seasoning
⅛ teaspoon pepper
1 stewing chicken (4 to 5 pounds), cut up
4 medium potatoes (about 1 pound), quartered
6 medium carrots, cut in pieces
¼ cup flour

Combine soup, 1 cup water, celery, onion, and seasonings in large heavy pan; add chicken. Cover; cook over low heat 1½ hours; stir often. Add vegetables. Cover; cook 45 minutes or until chicken and vegetables are tender. To thicken, blend flour and remaining water; gradually stir into stew. Cook 10 to 15 minutes; stir often. 4 to 6 servings.

DAY-AFTER TURKEY DIVAN

1 package (10 ounces) frozen broccoli or asparagus spears, cooked and drained
4 large slices turkey
1 can (10½ ounces) condensed cream of vegetable, celery, chicken, or mushroom soup
⅓ cup milk
½ cup shredded Cheddar cheese

Arrange broccoli in shallow baking dish (10 x 6 x 2"). Top with turkey slices. Blend soup and milk; pour over turkey; sprinkle with cheese. Bake in a 450° oven until sauce is slightly browned, about 15 minutes. 4 servings.

POULET AU VIN

2 pounds chicken parts
¼ cup butter or margarine
1 can (10½ ounces) condensed
  cream of mushroom soup
⅓ cup sherry (optional)
Dash pepper
10 small white onions

Brown chicken in butter in large skillet. Stir in soup, sherry, and pepper; add onions. Cover; simmer 45 minutes or until chicken is tender; stir often. 4 to 6 servings. (If desired, add ⅛ teaspoon whole thyme when browning chicken and substitute ⅓ cup water for sherry. Omit pepper.)

GOLDEN CHICKEN BAKE

2 packages (1 pound each) frozen
  chicken parts, thawed
2 tablespoons melted butter or
  margarine
1 can (10½ ounces) condensed
  Cheddar cheese, cream of
  vegetable, celery, chicken, or
  mushroom soup
¼ cup chopped toasted almonds

In shallow baking dish (12x8x2"), arrange chicken skin-side down. Pour butter over. Bake at 400°F. for 20 minutes. Turn chicken; bake 20 minutes more. Stir soup; pour over chicken; sprinkle with almonds. Bake 20 minutes more or until tender. Stir sauce before serving. 4 to 6 servings.

CHICKEN CROQUETTES WITH SAUCE

1 can (10½ ounces) condensed
  cream of chicken soup
1½ cups minced cooked chicken
¼ cup fine dry bread crumbs
2 tablespoons minced parsley
1 tablespoon finely minced onion
Bread crumbs
Shortening
¼ cup milk

Combine ⅓ cup soup with chicken, ¼ cup crumbs, parsley, and onion. Form into 6 croquettes; roll in bread crumbs. Chill. Fry croquettes in shortening until thoroughly heated and lightly browned. Blend remaining soup with milk; heat; serve over croquettes. 3 servings.

CREAMED CHICKEN

½ cup chopped celery
2 tablespoons butter or margarine
1 can (10½ ounces) condensed
  cream of chicken soup
⅓ to ½ cup milk
1 can (5 ounces) boned chicken or
  turkey, or 1 cup diced cooked
  chicken or turkey
1 cup cooked peas
⅛ teaspoon ground sage

Cook celery in butter until tender. Blend in other ingredients. Heat; stir often. Serve over split corn bread squares, biscuits, or toast. 3 servings.

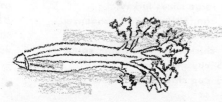

CHICKEN A LA KING

¼ cup chopped onion
2 tablespoons chopped green
 pepper
2 tablespoons butter or margarine
1 can (10½ ounces) condensed
 cream of chicken or mushroom
 soup
⅓ to ½ cup milk
1 cup cubed cooked chicken, ham,
 or turkey
2 tablespoons diced pimiento
Dash pepper
Toast

Cook onion and green pepper in butter until tender. Blend in soup and milk; add chicken, pimiento, and pepper. Heat slowly; stir often. Serve over toast. 4 servings.

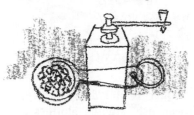

CHICKEN LIVERS IN PATTY SHELLS

1 package (8 ounces) frozen
 chicken livers
2 tablespoons butter or margarine
½ cup chopped celery
¼ cup chopped onion
1 can (10½ ounces) condensed
 cream of chicken or mushroom
 soup
⅓ cup milk
¼ teaspoon paprika
4 patty shells

Cook livers slowly in butter or margarine in covered skillet until thawed and browned; stir often. Add celery and onion; cook until tender. Gradually blend in soup, milk, and paprika. Heat; stir often. Serve in patty shells. 4 servings.

1-2-3 CHICKEN PIE

1 cup cubed cooked chicken
1 cup cubed cooked potatoes
½ cup cooked carrots (cut in strips),
 peas, or cut green beans
1 can (10½ ounces) condensed
 cream of chicken soup
¼ cup milk
1 tablespoon minced onion
Dash poultry seasoning
1 cup packaged biscuit mix
⅓ cup milk

Layer chicken and vegetables in a 1½-quart casserole. Blend soup, milk, onion, and poultry seasoning; pour over chicken and vegetables. Bake in a 450° oven 10 minutes. Meanwhile, combine biscuit mix and milk; roll ½-inch thick and cut into 6 or 7 biscuits. Remove casserole from oven; place biscuits on top. Continue baking 15 minutes or until biscuits are browned. 3 to 4 servings. A "1-2-3 Pie" may also be made with cream of mushroom soup and cooked beef or pork.

Savory Stuffings

Whether in a holiday turkey, large roasting chicken, or a fresh or frozen fish, stuffing glorifies a hearty main dish, and makes a feast. It's the cook's secret that this moist and flavorful family favorite is thrifty, too.

OLD-FASHIONED POULTRY STUFFING

8 cups bread cubes
1 cup chopped celery
½ cup finely chopped onion
¼ to ½ teaspoon poultry seasoning
Dash pepper
¼ cup butter or margarine
1 can (10½ ounces) condensed cream of celery, chicken, or mushroom soup

Brown bread cubes on cookie sheet at 350°F. for 5 minutes. In skillet, cook celery and onion with seasonings in butter until vegetables are tender. Add soup; mix lightly with bread. Spoon into 1½-quart casserole. Bake at 350°F. for 45 minutes. Makes 6 cups stuffing.

OVERSTUFFED CHICKEN

2 cans (10½ ounces each) condensed golden mushroom soup
⅔ cup water
1 package (8 ounces) herb-seasoned stuffing
2 broilers (about 2½ pounds each), split
Paprika
⅓ cup chopped onion
Generous dash poultry seasoning
2 tablespoons butter or margarine

Combine soup with water. In roasting pan (15x10½"), mix ⅔ cup soup mixture with stuffing mix; spread in pan. Arrange broilers over stuffing, sprinkle with paprika. Cover; bake at 400°F. for 30 minutes. Uncover, bake 45 minutes longer or until tender. Meanwhile, in saucepan, cook onion with seasoning in butter until onion is tender. Stir in remaining soup mixture. Heat; stir now and then. Serve with chicken and stuffing. 4 servings.

OYSTER BAR STUFFING

¼ cup chopped celery
2 tablespoons chopped onion
2 tablespoons butter or margarine
1 can (10 ounces) frozen condensed
   oyster stew
6 cups dry bread cubes

Cook celery and onion in butter until tender. Add soup; heat until soup is thawed; mix lightly with bread cubes. Makes 4 cups stuffing or enough for a 3- to 4-pound bird.

SAVORY SAUSAGE STUFFING

½ pound sausage
1 small onion, chopped
1 can (10½ ounces) condensed
   cream of celery soup
8 cups dry bread cubes

Brown sausage; stir to separate meat particles. (If using link sausage, slice before browning.) Add onion; cook until tender. Blend in soup; mix lightly with bread cubes. Makes about 6 cups stuffing, or enough for a 5- to 6-pound bird.

DEEP SOUTH STUFFING

½ cup chopped onion
2 cups chopped celery
6 tablespoons butter or margarine
5 cups corn bread crumbs (one 12-
   ounce package corn muffin mix,
   baked as directed)
3 cups dry bread cubes
1 teaspoon poultry seasoning
1 can (10½ ounces) condensed
   cream of chicken soup
¼ cup milk

Cook onion and celery in butter until tender. Combine with corn bread crumbs, bread cubes, and poultry seasoning. Blend soup and milk; pour over bread mixture; mix lightly. Makes about 8 cups stuffing or enough for an 8- to 10-pound turkey.

DUTCH COUNTRY STUFFING

1 can (10½ ounces) condensed
   beef broth
2 cups chopped apple
¾ cup chopped onion
½ cup chopped celery
¼ cup sugar
2 tablespoons butter or margarine
¼ teaspoon ground sage
⅛ teaspoon ground nutmeg
Dash ground cinnamon
12 cups dry bread cubes

Combine all ingredients except bread cubes; simmer 10 minutes. Pour over bread cubes a little at a time, mixing well after each addition. Makes about 8 cups or enough stuffing for a 5- to 6-pound pork shoulder roast.

Fish and Seafood

Fish never tastes better than when brought to the table bubbling in a savory sauce.

Whether you catch your fish in the freezer or offshore, you can give it family-appeal flavor and extra color by these recipes. They include budget balancers and party spectaculars you'll treasure.

SAUCY FISH FILLETS

1 pound whitefish fillets
1 can (10½ ounces) condensed cream of mushroom soup
Topping: ½ cup shredded Cheddar cheese, chopped parsley, paprika, corn flakes, toast cubes, or thin lemon slices

If using frozen fish, thaw and blot dry first. Arrange in shallow baking dish (10 x 6 x 2"). Stir soup in can; pour over fish. Top as desired. Bake in a 400° oven 20 minutes. 4 servings. VARIATION: Use cream of celery soup in place of cream of mushroom.

SEASIDE STEW

1 can (4 ounces) sliced mushrooms, drained
1 tablespoon butter or margarine
1 can (10 ounces) frozen condensed cream of shrimp soup
½ cup light cream
2 to 3 cups cut-up cooked seafood (crab, white fish, lobster, scallops, shrimp)
¼ cup shredded sharp cheese
3 tablespoons sauterne (optional)

Brown mushrooms lightly in butter. Add soup and cream; heat slowly until soup is thawed. Blend in seafood and cheese. Heat; stir often. Add sauterne just before serving. Serve with hot buttered rice or noodles. 4 to 6 servings.

SHRIMP À LA KING

¼ cup chopped onion
1 can (4 ounces) sliced mushrooms, drained
2 tablespoons butter or margarine
1 can (10 ounces) frozen condensed cream of shrimp soup
½ cup milk
1 cup diced cooked shrimp
4 slices toast or 3 cups cooked rice

Cook onion and mushrooms in butter until onion is tender. Add soup, milk, and shrimp. Heat until soup is thawed; stir often. Serve over toast or rice. If desired, omit onion and mushrooms; substitute ¼ cup diced green pepper and 1 tablespoon chopped pimiento. 4 servings.

SHRIMP CREOLE

1 large green pepper, sliced
1 large onion, sliced
1 small clove garlic, minced
2 tablespoons shortening
1 can (10½ ounces) condensed tomato soup
⅓ cup water
2 teaspoons lemon juice
¼ teaspoon salt
Dash pepper
Dash "Tabasco" sauce
1 pound shrimp, cooked and cleaned (or two 6-ounce cans, drained)
3 cups cooked rice

Cook green pepper, onion, and garlic in shortening in covered skillet over low heat until tender. Stir in soup, water, lemon juice, seasonings, and shrimp. Cook about 10 minutes; stir often. Serve over rice. 4 to 6 servings.

LOBSTER-SHRIMP THERMIDOR

1 can (4 ounces) sliced mushrooms, drained
1 tablespoon butter or margarine
1 cup diced cooked lobster, or 1 can (6 ounces) lobster, drained
1 can (10 ounces) frozen condensed cream of shrimp soup
¼ cup milk
¼ teaspoon dry mustard
Dash cayenne pepper
Grated Parmesan cheese
Paprika

Brown mushrooms in butter. Add lobster and cook a few minutes. Stir in soup, milk, mustard, and cayenne. Heat slowly until soup is thawed; stir often. Spoon lobster mixture into 3 individual baking dishes. Sprinkle cheese and paprika on top. Bake in a 400° oven about 15 minutes. 3 servings.

GRATIN OF OYSTERS AND SPINACH

1 tablespoon chopped green onion
1 tablespoon butter or margarine
1 can (10 ounces) frozen condensed oyster stew
2 tablespoons flour
⅓ cup water
6 to 8 ounces thinly sliced Canadian bacon
2 packages (10 ounces each) frozen spinach, cooked and well drained
2 slices Swiss cheese

Cook green onion in butter until tender. Add soup; heat slowly until thawed; stir often. Blend flour and water to form a smooth paste; stir into hot soup. Cook; stir often until soup thickens. Meanwhile, broil bacon in a large shallow baking dish or heat-proof skillet. Top bacon with spinach; pour soup sauce over. Place cheese on sauce; broil until melted. 4 servings.

BARBECUE-BAKED FISH

1 pound fish fillets (thaw if frozen)
1 tablespoon butter or margarine
4 thin slices lemon
4 thin onion rings
2 tablespoons chopped parsley
1 can (10¾ ounces) condensed tomato soup
¼ cup water

In baking dish (10x6x2″) place fish; sprinkle with salt, pepper. Dot with butter; top with lemon, onion, parsley. Mix soup, water; pour over fish. Bake at 350°F. for 20 minutes or until done. 4 servings.

DEVILED CRAB

1 can (10½ ounces) condensed cream of celery soup
1 cup flaked cooked crab, or 1 can (7 ounces), drained
2 tablespoons chopped green pepper
1 tablespoon chopped onion
2 teaspoons lemon juice
1 teaspoon Worcestershire
½ teaspoon prepared mustard
2 tablespoons buttered bread crumbs

Combine all ingredients, except bread crumbs; spoon into 4 small buttered baking dishes. (Clam shells are attractive for this.) Sprinkle crumbs over crab mixture. Bake in a 350° oven 20 minutes or until lightly browned. 4 servings.

OYSTERS A LA QUEEN

1 can (10 ounces) frozen condensed
oyster stew
2 tablespoons butter or margarine
1 can (4 ounces) sliced mushrooms,
drained
¼ cup minced onion
2 tablespoons flour
¼ cup milk
2 tablespoons diced pimiento
4 slices buttered toast

Thaw soup just before using by placing unopened can in pan of hot water for about 30 minutes. Meanwhile, melt butter in saucepan; add mushrooms and onion; brown lightly. Stir in flour to make a smooth paste. Blend in oyster stew, milk, and pimiento. Heat; stir constantly until smooth and slightly thickened. Serve over toast. 3 to 4 servings.

CREAMED SALMON

¼ cup chopped onion
1 tablespoon butter or margarine
1 can (10½ ounces) condensed
cream of mushroom or celery soup
⅓ to ½ cup milk
1 can (8 ounces) salmon, or 1 can
(7 ounces) tuna, drained and
flaked
¾ cup cooked green beans
1 tablespoon lemon juice (optional)

Cook onion in butter until tender. Blend in soup, milk, fish, green beans, and lemon juice. Heat; stir often. Serve over toast or rice. 3 to 4 servings.

SEAFOOD AU GRATIN

1 can (11 ounces) condensed
Cheddar cheese soup
¼ cup milk
2 cups cooked seafood (shrimp, lobster, crab, white fish, or any combination of these)
1 tablespoon chopped parsley
¼ cup buttered bread crumbs

In 1-quart casserole, stir soup until smooth; gradually add milk. Mix in seafood and parsley. Top with bread crumbs. Bake in a 400° oven 30 minutes or until bubbling. 3 to 4 servings.

SEAFOOD NEWBURG

1 can (10 ounces) frozen condensed
cream of shrimp soup
⅓ to ½ cup milk
1 cup flaked cooked lobster or 1
can (6 ounces) lobster, drained
and flaked
1 tablespoon sauterne (optional)
Cooked rice

Heat soup and milk slowly until soup is thawed. Add lobster and sauterne. Heat a few minutes more; stir often. Serve over rice. 4 servings.

Saucery

Lucky the housewife who discovers the versatile sauces always on hand in cans of condensed soup. Whether you're adding new flavor appeal to leftover meat or preparing gravy for a chicken, a can of soup is ready to fill your sauce-making needs with magical ease.

White sauce or cream sauce comes all blended for you in a can of cream soup. Whenever a recipe calls for white sauce, take a can of soup. Choose the one with the extra-special flavor you want—cream of vegetable, chicken, mushroom, or celery soup. Simply add a little liquid to thin the soup sauce to the thickness you prefer, and use it as a pour-on cream sauce.

Gravy, also, is always available in the cream soups. Just blend with a little liquid and/or drippings for the kind of gravy menfolk applaud.

VERSATILE CREAM SAUCE

1 can (10½ ounces) condensed Cheddar cheese, cream of vegetable, celery, chicken, or mushroom soup
¼ to ½ cup milk

Pour soup into pan. Stir to blend. Add milk. Heat; stir often. Makes about 1½ cups sauce. Use for creaming vegetables and meats.

INSTANT CHEESE SAUCE: Pour 1 can Cheddar cheese soup into pan. Stir contents well to blend. Stir in ¼ to ⅓ cup milk. Heat slowly, stirring often.

4-WAY CHEESE SAUCE: Pour 1 can any cream soup into pan. Stir to blend. Add ¼ to ½ cup milk and ½ cup shredded Cheddar cheese. Heat; stir often.

Type Sauce	Use 1 can Soup	Add and Heat
Almond for chicken, veal, seafood	Cream of chicken or mushroom	⅓ cup water, ¼ cup chopped almonds and 1 tablespoon minced onion browned in butter; 1 tablespoon sherry (optional)
Creamy Cheese for vegetables or chicken	Cream of celery or cream of vegetable	Blend 3-ounce package of softened cream cheese with soup before adding ¼ to ⅓ cup milk
Curry for chicken, veal, lamb, or seafood	Cream of asparagus, celery, or chicken	¼ to ⅓ cup milk and ¼ to 1 teaspoon curry powder
Herb for chicken, fish, veal, vegetables, eggs	Cream of celery, chicken, or mushroom	¼ to ½ cup milk and dash of basil, marjoram, poultry seasoning, sage, or thyme
Nut for chicken, veal, or vegetables	Cream of mushroom	⅓ to ½ cup milk and ¼ cup chopped walnuts or other nuts
Parsley for fish, eggs, vegetables	Cream of vegetable or celery	¼ to ⅓ cup milk and 1 tablespoon chopped parsley
Pimiento-Egg for fish	Cream of celery	⅓ cup water, 1 tablespoon chopped onion browned in butter, 1 hard-cooked egg (chopped), 2 tablespoons chopped pimiento
Poulette for chicken or fish	Cream of chicken	¼ to ⅓ cup milk and 2 tablespoons minced onion browned in butter, 2 tablespoons chopped parsley, 2 teaspoons lemon juice, and 1 to 2 tablespoons sherry (optional)
Sour Cream for beef, chicken, fish	Cream of mushroom	¼ to ½ cup water, 2 tablespoons chopped onion browned in butter, ¼ cup sour cream, ⅛ teaspoon paprika

TOMATO SOUP SAUCE

Plain Sauce: Heat tomato soup just as it comes from the can. You may want to thin it a bit by adding a little water. Season as you like—with prepared mustard or horseradish, Worcestershire, "Tabasco" sauce, lemon juice, or herb such as thyme or oregano. 1¼ cups sauce. Use as a pour-on for: Pork chops, beef patties, corned beef hash, frankfurters, or fish sticks.

Tomato Horseradish Sauce: Stir in 2 tablespoons prepared horseradish, 1 tablespoon prepared mustard, dash of ground cloves, and pepper. 1½ cups sauce. Serve with beef, ham, frankfurters, or meat loaf.

Tomato Cheese Sauce: Add ⅓ cup milk and ½ cup shredded Cheddar cheese. Heat; stir often until cheese is melted. 1⅔ cups sauce. Serve with fish, omelet, or vegetables.

EGG CHEESE SAUCE

1 can (11 ounces) condensed
  Cheddar cheese soup
¼ cup milk
1 hard-cooked egg, sliced
¼ teaspoon prepared mustard

Stir soup until smooth. Gradually blend in milk; add egg and mustard. Heat; stir often. 1½ cups sauce. Serve over cooked broccoli or cauliflower.

SAUCE CREVETTES

1 tablespoon chopped green onion
1 tablespoon chopped ripe olives
Dash leaf thyme
1 tablespoon butter or margarine
1 can (10 ounces) frozen condensed
  cream of shrimp soup
⅓ to ½ cup milk

Cook green onion, olives, and thyme in butter until onion is tender. Add soup and milk. Heat until thawed; stir often. Serve over 6 poached eggs on toast or over cooked shrimp. 6 servings.

CREAMY TOMATO SAUCE

¼ cup chopped onion
⅛ teaspoon leaf thyme
1 tablespoon butter or margarine
1 can (10½ ounces) condensed
   tomato soup
½ cup sour cream
¼ cup water
2 teaspoons paprika
¼ teaspoon salt
Dash pepper

Cook onion and thyme in butter until onion is tender. Blend in remaining ingredients. Heat; stir often. Makes 2 cups sauce. Serve with chicken or veal.

SHRIMP-FISH SAUCE

¼ cup chopped cucumber
2 tablespoons chopped onion
2 tablespoons butter or margarine
1 can (10 ounces) frozen condensed
   cream of shrimp soup
⅓ cup milk
1 to 2 teaspoons lemon juice

Cook cucumber and onion in butter until just tender. Add remaining ingredients. Heat until soup is thawed; stir often. 1¾ cups sauce. Serve over baked fish.

HERB CHEESE SAUCE

1 can (10½ ounces) condensed
   cream of mushroom soup
⅓ to ½ cup milk
1 cup shredded Cheddar cheese
1 tablespoon chopped parsley
Generous dash tarragon, crushed

Stir soup until smooth; blend in milk. Add remaining ingredients. Heat; stir often. 2 cups sauce. Serve over cooked peas and onions, green beans, or broccoli.

STROGANOFF SAUCE

¼ cup chopped onion
½ teaspoon paprika
2 tablespoons butter or margarine
1 can (10½ ounces) condensed
   golden mushroom soup
¼ cup sour cream

In saucepan, cook onion with paprika in butter until tender. Stir in soup and sour cream. Heat; stir now and then. Makes 1½ cups sauce. Serve with beef patties or sliced cooked beef or veal.

SPAGHETTI WITH CLAM-OYSTER SAUCE

1 clove garlic, minced
½ cup chopped onion
¼ cup chopped parsley
2 tablespoons olive oil
1 can (10 ounces) frozen condensed
   oyster stew
1 can (7½ ounces) minced clams,
   drained
2 teaspoons lemon juice
½ pound thin spaghetti

Cook garlic, onion, and parsley in olive oil until onion is tender. Add oyster stew, clams, and lemon juice. Heat until soup is thawed; stir now and then. Meanwhile, cook spaghetti in boiling salted water; drain. Then heap into 4 to 6 soup bowls. Ladle the sauce (sauce is very thin) over. 2 cups sauce.

SPAGHETTI SAUCE WITH MEAT

½ pound ground beef
½ cup chopped onion
1 teaspoon leaf oregano, crushed
1 large clove garlic, minced
1 can (10½ ounces) condensed
   tomato soup
½ soup can water
1 tablespoon vinegar
Cooked spaghetti
   (6 ounces uncooked)

Lightly brown ground beef and cook onion with oregano and garlic in skillet. Add remaining ingredients except spaghetti. Cover. Cook over low heat 30 minutes. Stir often. Serve over hot spaghetti. 3 to 4 servings.

WHITE CLAM SAUCE

1 can (7½ ounces) minced clams,
   drained
1 medium clove garlic, minced
2 tablespoons butter or margarine
1 can (10½ ounces) condensed
   cream of mushroom soup
½ cup water
2 tablespoons chopped parsley
½ pound spaghetti, cooked

In saucepan, cook clams and garlic in butter a few minutes. Stir in soup, water, and parsley. Heat; stir now and then. Serve over spaghetti. 4 servings.

CELERY-CAPER SAUCE FOR COLD MEAT

1 can (10½ ounces) condensed
   cream of celery soup
¼ cup mayonnaise
1 tablespoon capers

Place unopened can of soup in refrigerator 3 to 4 hours. Blend soup and mayonnaise; stir in capers. Serve with cold cooked salmon, sliced beef, or ham. 1½ cups sauce.

VARIATIONS:

Dill Sauce: Substitute 1 teaspoon lemon juice and ½ teaspoon dried dill leaves for capers. Serve with cold cooked salmon. 1½ cups sauce.

Horseradish Sauce: Substitute 1 to 2 teaspoons horseradish for capers. Serve with cold sliced beef or ham. 1½ cups sauce.

Mustard Sauce: Substitute 1 teaspoon mustard for capers. Serve with cold sliced beef or ham. 1½ cups sauce.

SAUCE A L'ORANGE

1 tablespoon chopped onion
2 tablespoons butter, margarine, or
   drippings
1 can (10½ ounces) condensed
   cream of mushroom soup
⅓ cup orange juice
1 teaspoon grated orange rind
⅛ teaspoon ground ginger

Brown onion in shortening. Blend in remaining ingredients; stir until smooth. Heat. 1½ cups sauce. Especially good with roast duck.

ZESTY TOMATO TOPPER FOR EGGS

¼ pound sausage links, thinly sliced
¼ cup chopped onion
2 tablespoons chopped green
   pepper
1 can (10¾ ounces) condensed
   tomato rice soup
½ cup water
1 tablespoon dry red wine
   (optional)

Cook sausage slices until lightly browned; pour off excess drippings. Add onion and green pepper; cook until tender. Blend in remaining ingredients. Cook over low heat 10 minutes; stir often. 4 servings. Serve over omelet or scrambled eggs.

ALMOND CHEESE SAUCE

1 can (11 ounces) condensed
   Cheddar cheese soup
¼ cup milk
¼ cup slivered almonds
¼ teaspoon curry powder

Stir soup until smooth. Gradually blend in milk; add remaining ingredients. Heat; stir often. 1½ cups sauce. Serve over cooked broccoli or cauliflower.

QUICK TOULONNAISE SAUCE

2 tablespoons chopped green
   onion
⅛ teaspoon savory
1 tablespoon butter or margarine
1 can (10¾ ounces) condensed
   cream of vegetable soup
⅓ cup milk
1 tablespoon Chablis or other dry
   white wine (optional)

Cook green onion and savory in butter until green onion is tender. Blend in remaining ingredients. Heat; stir often. 1½ cups sauce. Serve over asparagus.

TANGY FISH SAUCE

¼ cup chopped celery
1 small clove garlic, minced
2 tablespoons butter or margarine
1 can (10 ounces) frozen condensed
   cream of shrimp soup
⅓ cup milk
1 to 2 tablespoons chopped dill
   pickle
⅛ teaspoon dry mustard

Cook celery and garlic in butter until celery is tender. Add remaining ingredients. Heat until soup is thawed; stir often. 1½ cups sauce. Serve over frozen prepared fried seafood or fried fish fillets.

MOCK HOLLANDAISE

1 can (10½ ounces) condensed
   cream of vegetable, celery,
   chicken, or mushroom soup
½ cup milk
2 tablespoons butter or margarine
2 tablespoons lemon juice
2 egg yolks, slightly beaten

Combine all ingredients. Heat over low heat just until thickened, stirring constantly. *Do not boil.* 1⅔ cups sauce. Serve with cooked vegetables or fish.

EASY HOLLANDAISE: Use any cream soup. Omit milk, butter, and egg yolks. Reduce lemon juice to 1 tablespoon and add ¼ cup mayonnaise.

SAUCE CREOLE

1 small green pepper, sliced
1 small onion, sliced
1 can (4 ounces) sliced mushrooms,
   drained
2 tablespoons butter or margarine
1 can (10½ ounces) condensed
   tomato soup
¼ cup water
1 teaspoon vinegar

Cook green pepper, onion, and mushrooms in butter until tender. Stir in remaining ingredients. Cook over low heat 5 minutes. 2 cups sauce. Serve over omelet, hamburgers, or baked fish.

SOUPER GRAVY

1 can (10½ ounces) condensed cream of vegetable, celery, chicken, or mushroom soup
¼ to ⅓ cup water
2 to 4 tablespoons drippings or butter

When preparing gravy for roast or fried meat, remove meat from pan and pour off and measure drippings. Pour can of soup into pan; stir well to loosen browned bits. Blend in water and drippings for thickness desired. Heat; stir often. 1½ cups gravy. Serve with fried chicken, roast beef, roast pork, pork chops, hamburgers, or baked ham.

QUICK ONION GRAVY

1 cup sliced onion
1 small clove garlic, minced
3 tablespoons butter or margarine
1 can (10½ ounces) condensed golden mushroom soup
½ cup water

In saucepan, cook onion and garlic in butter until tender. Stir in soup and water. Heat; stir now and then. Serve over beef patties or sliced cooked beef or pork.

CREAMY GIBLET GRAVY

4 ounces chicken giblets, chopped and cooked
½ cup chopped celery
2 tablespoons butter or margarine
1 can (10½ ounces) condensed cream of chicken soup
⅓ cup water

Brown giblets and cook celery in butter until tender. Blend in remaining ingredients. Heat; stir often. 2 cups gravy.

Barbecue Bonanza

Catch a whiff of meat or poultry barbecuing! That's the call to good eating . . . for barbecues can be held inside (on a rotisserie, in the oven, on a hibachi in the fireplace, or even in a skillet on top of the range), or outdoors on plain or fancy grills. Whatever the location, it's smart to reach for the soup can for rare finds in easy, zesty sauces when the cook moves to preparation of a barbecue.

An easy reputation as a barbecue chef is yours with a good sauce, good brush (long-handled or pastry), and a cut of meat which turns crisp and luscious over carefully controlled heat. Select your recipe from the following pages.

ALL 'ROUND TOMATO BARBECUE SAUCE

1 can (10½ ounces) condensed tomato soup
2 to 4 tablespoons sweet pickle relish
¼ cup chopped onion
1 tablespoon brown sugar
1 tablespoon vinegar
1 tablespoon Worcestershire

Combine all ingredients. Cover; simmer until onion is cooked and flavors are blended. 1½ cups sauce.

BARBECUED FRANKFURTERS

SKILLET: Combine sauce as directed. Add 1 pound frankfurters. Cover; simmer 20 minutes; stir often. 4 to 5 servings.

OUTDOOR COOKING: Prepare sauce as directed. Slit 2 pounds frankfurters lengthwise; brush with sauce. Place on grill over glowing coals. Cook, brushing with sauce and turning every few minutes, until nicely browned. 8 to 10 servings.

BARBECUED HAMBURGERS

SKILLET: Shape 2 pounds seasoned ground beef into 8 patties. Brown in butter or margarine. Add sauce ingredients. Simmer until patties are done. 8 servings.

OUTDOOR COOKING: Prepare sauce as directed. Make patties as in skillet method. Place on grill about 6 inches above glowing coals. Cook about 15 minutes, brushing with sauce and turning every 5 minutes. 8 servings.

BARBECUED CHICKEN

SKILLET: Brown 2 pounds chicken parts in 2 to 4 tablespoons butter or margarine. Add sauce ingredients. Cover; simmer 45 minutes or until chicken is done. Stir now and then. 4 to 6 servings.

OUTDOOR COOKING: Combine sauce ingredients. Divide 2 pounds chicken parts on sheets of double thickness heavy duty aluminum foil (about 2 or 3 pieces chicken per sheet). Spread with about ¼ cup of sauce. Fold foil over; bring edges together; seal tightly with double fold. Cook on grill 4 to 5 inches above bed of hot coals 40 to 45 minutes. Turn packets over now and then. 4 to 6 servings.

BARBECUED STEAK

OUTDOOR COOKING: Prepare sauce. Place steak (2 pounds, cut ¾-inch thick) on grill about 6 inches above glowing coals. Brush with sauce; cook 10 minutes. Turn; brush with sauce. Cook 10 minutes longer or until desired doneness. Heat remaining sauce. Serve with steak. 4 to 6 servings.

SAUCE FOR BARBECUE SANDWICHES

⅓ cup chopped green onion
1 tablespoon chopped hot cherry
    peppers
2 tablespoons butter or margarine
1 can (10½ ounces) condensed
    tomato soup
¼ cup water
1 tablespoon brown sugar
1 teaspoon prepared horseradish

Cook onion and peppers in butter until onion is tender. Add remaining ingredients. Simmer 15 minutes or until flavors are blended; stir often. 1⅓ cups sauce.

FRANK SANDWICHES

Prepare sauce. Slit 1 pound frankfurters lengthwise. Place on broiler pan; brush with sauce. Broil about 3 inches from heat until done, brushing with sauce and turning often. Serve on toasted buns. 4 to 5 servings.

BURGER SANDWICHES

Prepare sauce. Shape 1½ pounds seasoned ground beef into 6 patties. Place on broiler pan; brush with sauce. Broil about 3 inches from heat until done, brushing with sauce and turning often. Serve on toasted buns. 6 servings.

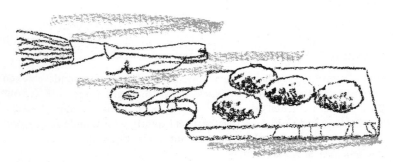

SPEEDY BARBECUE SAUCE

1 can (10½ ounces) condensed
    onion soup
½ cup ketchup
2 tablespoons salad oil
1 large clove garlic, minced
4 drops "Tabasco" sauce
¼ teaspoon salt
Dash pepper

Combine all ingredients. Cover; simmer 10 minutes; stir often. 2 cups sauce. Use sauce for basting hamburgers, frankfurters, chicken, or spareribs. Serve extra sauce over meats.

ONION BARBECUE SAUCE

1 can (10½ ounces) condensed
cream of mushroom soup
1 can (10½ ounces) condensed
onion soup
½ cup ketchup
¼ cup salad oil
¼ cup vinegar
2 large cloves garlic, minced
2 tablespoons brown sugar
1 tablespoon Worcestershire
⅛ teaspoon "Tabasco" sauce

Combine all ingredients. Cover; simmer 15 minutes; stir often. 3⅓ cups sauce. Use for chicken, ribs.

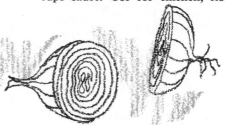

OUTDOOR CHICKEN

Prepare sauce. Brush 4 split broilers with salad oil. Place on grill (skin-side up) about 6 inches above glowing coals. Cook 15 minutes; turn; cook 15 minutes more. Brush with sauce; continue cooking 30 minutes or until chicken is done, brushing with sauce and turning every 5 minutes. 8 servings.

OUTDOOR SPARERIBS

Place 6 pounds spareribs (cut into serving-size pieces) in a large pot of boiling water. Cover; simmer 1 hour; drain. Prepare sauce as directed. Place ribs on grill about 6 inches above glowing coals. Brush with sauce; continue cooking 30 minutes or until done, brushing with sauce and turning every 5 minutes. 6 servings.

OVEN BARBECUED SPARERIBS

4 pounds spareribs, cut in serving-
size pieces
1 can (10½ ounces) condensed
beef broth
1½ cups mincemeat
3 tablespoons vinegar

Place spareribs in roasting pan (13 x 9 x 2"). Bake in a 350° oven 1 hour; pour off fat. Combine remaining ingredients; pour over ribs. Bake 1½ hours more or until done; baste now and then. 4 to 6 servings.

OUTDOOR CHICKEN OR SPARERIBS

Prepare sauce. Use 2 split broilers or 4 pounds spareribs. Follow cooking directions for outdoor chicken or spareribs in Onion Barbecue Sauce recipe. 4 servings.

BARBECUED LAMB KABOBS

1 can (10½ ounces) condensed
   tomato soup
1 small clove garlic, minced
2 tablespoons salad oil
2 tablespoons wine vinegar
1 tablespoon sugar
½ teaspoon salt
⅛ teaspoon pepper
⅛ teaspoon leaf oregano, crushed
Dash leaf thyme
1 pound leg of lamb, cut in
   1½-inch cubes
1 medium green pepper, cut in
   1½-inch pieces
1 medium onion, cut in ½-inch
   slices

Blend soup, garlic, oil, vinegar, sugar, and seasonings. Add lamb; stir until well coated. Cover; place in refrigerator 4 hours. On 4 skewers arrange alternately lamb, green pepper, and onion. Place on broiler rack. Brush kabobs with sauce. Broil about 3 inches from heat for 30 minutes or until meat is tender. Brush kabobs with sauce and turn every 3 or 4 minutes. 4 servings.

NOTE: To cook outdoors: Prepare kabobs as directed above. Place on grill about 4 to 5 inches above glowing coals. Brush kabobs with sauce. Cook 25 to 30 minutes or until meat is tender, brushing with sauce and turning every few minutes. 4 servings.

SKILLET BARBECUED CHICKEN

2 pounds chicken parts
½ teaspoon salt
Dash pepper
¼ cup butter or margarine
1 can (10½ ounces) condensed
   tomato soup
½ cup chopped onion
3 tablespoons wine vinegar
2 tablespoons brown sugar
1 tablespoon Worcestershire
Dash sweet basil
Dash leaf thyme
5 drops "Tabasco" sauce

Season chicken with salt and pepper; brown in butter. Stir in remaining ingredients. Cover. Cook over low heat 45 minutes or until chicken is tender; stir now and then. 4 to 6 servings.

Vegetables with New Flavor

There are new ways to interest your family in vegetables! Reach for a can of soup.

Whether you cook a mixture of garden vegetables French style in clear consomme, or dish up a casserole of green beans baked to creamy perfection, your family will cheer these dishes they often otherwise neglect.

Here are the easiest ways in the world to cook flavorful creamed onions, add unexpected tang and color to baked potatoes, prepare scalloped potatoes that will get rave requests for seconds. Try creaming all kinds of vegetables in soup.

VEGETABLE CHEESE BAKE

1 large bunch broccoli or head
cauliflower (or two 10-ounce
packages frozen) cooked
and drained
1 can (10½ ounces) condensed
cream of vegetable, celery,
chicken, or mushroom soup
⅓ to ½ cup milk
½ cup shredded sharp Cheddar
cheese
¼ cup buttered bread crumbs

Place broccoli or cauliflower in shallow baking dish (10 x 6 x 2"). Blend soup, milk, and cheese; pour over vegetable. Top with crumbs. Bake in a 350° oven 30 minutes or until bubbling. 6 to 8 servings.

EASY CREAMED VEGETABLES

Top-of-stove method: Cook 2 packages (10 ounces each) frozen vegetables (cauliflower, corn, green beans, lima beans, mixed vegetables, peas, peas and carrots, spinach) in unsalted water until tender; drain. Stir in 1 can condensed cream of vegetable, celery, chicken, mushroom, or Cheddar cheese soup; heat. Thin to desired consistency with additional milk. Season to taste. 6 to 8 servings.

SAVORY POTATOES

2 slices bacon
½ cup chopped onion
1 can (10½ ounces) condensed cream of mushroom soup
Dash pepper
⅓ cup milk
5 cups cubed cooked potatoes

In saucepan, cook bacon until crisp; remove and crumble. Pour off all but 2 tablespoons drippings. Cook onion in drippings until tender. Stir in soup and pepper; gradually blend in milk. Add potatoes. Heat; stir now and then. 6 to 8 servings.

SCALLOPED POTATOES

1 can (10½ ounces) condensed Cheddar cheese, cream of vegetable, celery, chicken, or mushroom soup
½ to ¾ cup milk
Dash pepper
4 cups thinly sliced potatoes
1 small onion, thinly sliced
1 tablespoon butter or margarine
Dash paprika

Blend soup, milk, and pepper. Arrange alternate layers of potatoes, onion, and sauce in 1½-quart casserole. Dot top with butter; sprinkle with paprika. Cover; bake in a 375° oven 1 hour. Uncover; bake 15 minutes more. 4 to 6 servings.

NOTE: Sliced cooked potatoes may be substituted for raw potatoes. Mince onion and reduce cooking time to about 30 minutes; bake uncovered.

SHRIMP AND CRAB STUFFED POTATOES

1 can (10 ounces) frozen condensed cream of shrimp soup
¼ cup milk
1 tablespoon grated onion
Dash pepper
½ cup shredded sharp Cheddar cheese
4 medium Idaho potatoes, baked
1 can (7 ounces) crab meat, cleaned and flaked (about 1 cup)
Paprika

Combine soup, milk, onion, and pepper. Heat slowly; stir often. Add cheese; stir until melted. Cut potatoes in half lengthwise. Scoop out insides; place in bowl. Add soup mixture slowly; mix until blended and fluffy. Fold in crab meat. Spoon into potato shells. Bake on cookie sheet in a 450° oven 15 minutes. Sprinkle with paprika. 4 servings.

Barbecued Lamb Kabobs   Page 64

CREAMED ONIONS AND PEAS

1 can (10½ ounces) condensed
  cream of chicken or mushroom
  soup
⅓ cup milk
1 package (10 ounces) frozen peas,
  cooked and drained
12 cooked small white onions (or
  1-pound can), drained
Dash pepper

Blend soup and milk; add peas,
onion, and pepper. Heat; stir often.
4 to 6 servings.
NOTE: If desired, substitute 2 cups
cubed cooked potatoes (or 1-pound
can, drained), for onions. Decrease
milk to ¼ cup.

VEGETABLES IN CHEESE SAUCE

2 packages (10 ounces each) frozen
  broccoli or cauliflower, cooked
  and drained
1 can (11 ounces) condensed
  Cheddar cheese soup
¼ cup milk
¼ cup buttered bread crumbs

Place broccoli in shallow baking
dish (10 x 6 x 2"). Blend soup and
milk; pour over broccoli. Top with
crumbs. Bake in a 350° oven about
30 minutes or until hot and bubbling. 6 to 8 servings.

ONIONS AMANDINE

1 can (10½ ounces) condensed
  cream of celery or mushroom soup
4 cups cooked small white onions
  (or two 1-pound cans), drained
½ cup shredded Cheddar cheese
¼ cup chopped toasted almonds

Stir soup until smooth; mix with
onions in 1½-quart casserole.
Sprinkle cheese and nuts on top.
Bake in a 375° oven 30 minutes.
6 servings.
NOTE: If desired, substitute cashews,
peanuts, or pecans for almonds.

Seafood Curry   Page 92
Eggs Goldenrod   Page 75
Hurry Up Pork Hash   Page 36

BUTTER BEAN ZESTY BAKE

2 tablespoons chopped onion
2 tablespoons chopped green
  pepper
1 tablespoon butter or margarine
1 can (10½ ounces) condensed
  tomato soup
¼ cup water
1 tablespoon brown sugar
1 tablespoon vinegar
1 teaspoon prepared mustard
2 cans (1 pound each) butter beans,
  drained

Brown onion and green pepper in butter. Add remaining ingredients except beans. Heat. Put beans in buttered 1-quart casserole; pour sauce over. Bake in a 375° oven 45 minutes. 4 to 6 servings.

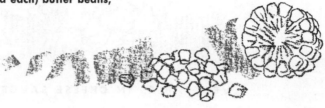

CREAMY CORN SCALLOP

1 can (10½ ounces) condensed
  cream of vegetable, celery,
  chicken, or mushroom soup
1 tablespoon minced onion
Dash pepper
1 can (1 pound) whole kernel corn,
  drained
1 cup crumbled soda crackers
2 tablespoons butter or margarine

Combine soup, onion, and pepper. In 1-quart casserole, arrange alternate layers of corn, soup mixture, and crackers; dot with butter. Bake in a 400° oven 25 minutes. 6 servings.

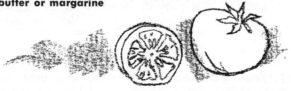

SUMMERTIME FRIED TOMATOES

4 medium tomatoes, sliced
⅓ cup seasoned flour
¼ cup butter or margarine
1 can (10½ ounces) condensed
  cream of mushroom soup
⅓ cup milk

Dip tomato slices in seasoned flour. Cook in butter over low heat until lightly browned on both sides. Remove to heated platter. Stir soup and milk into skillet. Heat. Pour sauce over tomatoes. 4 to 6 servings.

GLAZED CARROTS

2 tablespoons chopped onion
1 tablespoon chopped parsley
2 tablespoons butter or margarine
8 medium carrots, cut in 1- to
1½-inch slices
1 can (10½ ounces) condensed
consomme
Dash ground nutmeg

Cook onion and parsley in butter about 5 minutes. Add remaining ingredients. Cover; cook over medium heat 25 minutes. Uncover; continue cooking 20 minutes or until carrots are tender and sauce thickens and glazes carrots. (Watch carefully during last few minutes to prevent sticking.) 4 servings.

NOTE: To shorten cooking time, cut carrots in ½-inch slices. Cook, uncovered, about 30 minutes.

ITALIAN EGGPLANT BAKE

1 medium eggplant, peeled and cut
in 1- to 1½-inch cubes
1 large onion, sliced
1 medium green pepper, sliced
½ small clove garlic, minced
1 teaspoon leaf oregano, crushed
¼ cup butter or margarine
1 can (10½ ounces) condensed
tomato soup
1 cup water
¼ teaspoon salt
Garlic croutons (see index)
Grated Parmesan cheese

Cook eggplant in boiling salted water for 3 minutes; drain and place in shallow baking dish (10 x 6 x 2"). Cook onion, green pepper, garlic, and oregano in butter until tender. Add soup, water, and salt. Heat; pour sauce over eggplant. Bake in a 350° oven 45 minutes; stir often. Remove eggplant from oven. Turn temperature up to 425°. Top eggplant with croutons; sprinkle with cheese. Return to oven; bake 15 minutes more. 6 servings.

GREEN BEAN CASSEROLE

1 can (10½ ounces) condensed
cream of chicken or mushroom
soup
1 teaspoon soy sauce
1 can (3½ ounces) French fried
onions
3 cups cooked French style green
beans (or two 10-ounce packages
frozen, or two 1-pound cans),
drained
Dash pepper

In 1-quart casserole, stir soup and soy sauce until smooth; mix in ½ can onions, beans, and pepper. Bake in a 350° oven 20 minutes or until bubbling. Top with remaining onions. Bake 5 minutes more. 6 servings.

Egg and Cheese Cookery

Eggs and cheese enjoy a reputation of true versatility. Excellence and simplicity reign where soup and eggs or cheese are combined for meatless meals.

Soup sauces enrich egg dishes, help make cheese fondues and casseroles full of flavor. When it comes to a souffle, you'll find you can make this "show-off" dish with any one of 5 kinds of soup—and have the finest results. If it's a cheese sauce you need, look in the Saucery section.

Remember, both eggs and cheese are delicate . . . neither should be cooked at high temperatures.

EGG CROQUETTES

1 can (10½ ounces) condensed cream of celery, chicken, or mushroom soup

8 hard-cooked eggs, sieved or very finely chopped

¼ cup fine dry bread crumbs

2 tablespoons minced parsley

2 tablespoons minced onion

½ teaspoon salt

Dash pepper

2 tablespoons shortening

⅓ cup milk

Mix ¼ cup soup with eggs, bread crumbs, parsley, onion, and seasonings; form into 6 croquettes. (If mixture is difficult to handle, chill before shaping.) Roll in additional bread crumbs. Fry croquettes slowly in shortening until browned. Meanwhile, combine remaining soup with milk. Heat. Serve as sauce over croquettes. 3 servings.

EASY CHEESE SOUFFLE

1 can (11 ounces) condensed
Cheddar cheese soup

6 eggs, separated

Heat soup in saucepan, stirring; remove from heat. Beat egg yolks until thick and lemon-colored; stir into soup. In large bowl, using clean egg beater, beat egg whites until stiff; fold soup mixture into egg whites. Pour into 1½-quart casserole. Bake in a 300° oven 1 to 1¼ hours or at 400° for 30 minutes. Serve immediately. 4 to 6 servings.

SOUPER CHEESE SOUFFLE

1 can (10½ ounces) condensed cream of vegetable, celery, chicken, or mushroom soup, or 1 can (10 ounces) frozen condensed cream of shrimp soup, thawed

1 cup shredded sharp process cheese

6 eggs, separated

Combine soup and cheese; heat slowly until cheese melts. Beat egg yolks until thick and lemon-colored; stir into soup mixture. Beat egg whites until stiff; fold soup mixture into egg whites. Pour into ungreased 2-quart casserole. Bake in a 300° oven 1 to 1¼ hours, or in a 400° oven 30 minutes. Serve immediately. 4 to 6 servings.

Try these additions to vary the basic souffle:

Shrimp Surprise Souffle: ½ cup minced cooked broccoli, well drained, ¼ teaspoon lemon juice, and a dash ground nutmeg to cream of shrimp soup-cheese mixture. Proceed as above.

Asparagus Souffle: ⅛ teaspoon ground nutmeg and ½ cup chopped cooked asparagus to cream of mushroom soup-cheese mixture. Proceed as above.

Ham-Mushroom Souffle: ¼ teaspoon chervil, ½ cup finely minced cooked ham, and 2 tablespoons chopped parsley to cream of mushroom soup-cheese mixture. Proceed as above.

RUM TUM DITTY

1 can (10½ ounces) condensed tomato soup

¼ cup water

1 cup shredded sharp Cheddar cheese

3 to 4 slices toast

Combine soup, water, and cheese. Cook over low heat; stir often until cheese is melted. Serve over toast. 3 to 4 servings. If desired, garnish with hard-cooked egg slices or sardines.

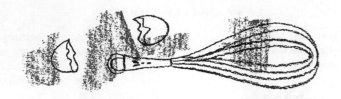

EASY EGGS BENEDICT

1 can (10½ ounces) condensed cream of vegetable, celery, chicken, or mushroom soup
⅓ cup milk
6 thin slices ham, fried
6 slices buttered toast or English muffin halves
6 eggs, poached
1 tablespoon minced parsley

Blend soup and milk. Heat. Meanwhile, place a slice of ham on each slice of toast or muffin half; top with poached egg. Pour sauce over eggs. Sprinkle with minced parsley. 6 servings.

SHRIMP OMELET

SAUCE:
1 can (10 ounces) frozen condensed cream of shrimp soup
½ cup milk
2 tablespoons chopped parsley
OMELET:
8 eggs
½ cup milk
¼ teaspoon salt
Dash pepper
4 tablespoons butter or margarine

For sauce, combine soup, milk, and parsley. Heat; stir now and then. For omelet, beat eggs, milk, and seasonings together. Heat butter in skillet; pour in egg mixture. Cook slowly. As undersurface becomes set, start lifting it slightly with spatula to let uncooked portion flow underneath and cook. When omelet is cooked but still moist, loosen edges and bottom. Pour sauce in center; fold one half over and roll omelet onto warm platter. 4 servings.

WESTERN RODEO OMELET

½ cup chopped cooked ham
¼ cup chopped green pepper
¼ cup chopped onion
¼ cup butter or margarine
1 can (10½ ounces) condensed cream of celery soup
8 eggs, slightly beaten

Cook ham, green pepper, and onion in butter until tender. Blend soup and eggs; add to ham and vegetables. Cook over low heat until eggs are set, lifting eggs gently now and then. 6 servings.

CREAMED EGGS

1 can (10½ ounces) condensed Cheddar cheese or cream of celery soup
⅓ to ½ cup milk
4 hard-cooked eggs, sliced
2 tablespoons chopped pimiento
4 slices toast

Blend soup and milk. Add eggs and pimiento. Heat; stir often. Serve on toast. 4 servings.

EGGS GOLDENROD: Omit pimiento. Separate cooked egg yolks and whites; chop whites coarsely; force yolks through a fine sieve. Add egg whites to heated sauce. Garnish each serving with sieved yolk.

BAKED CHEESE FONDUE

3 eggs, separated
1 can (10½ ounces) condensed cream of vegetable, celery, chicken, or mushroom soup
1 cup shredded sharp Cheddar or process cheese
¼ teaspoon dry mustard
2 cups small bread cubes

Beat egg whites until stiff but not dry. Beat egg yolks until thick. Blend in soup, cheese, and mustard; stir in bread cubes. Fold in egg whites. Spoon into 1½-quart casserole. Bake in a 325° oven 1 hour. 4 to 6 servings.

SWISS FONDUE

1 can (10 ounces) frozen condensed cream of shrimp soup
1 clove garlic
¼ cup Sauterne or other dry white wine
1½ cups shredded Swiss cheese
Dash nutmeg
French bread, cut in 1½-inch cubes

Place can of soup in pan of hot water for about 30 minutes to thaw. Rub saucepan with clove of garlic; discard garlic. In saucepan, combine soup, wine, cheese, and nutmeg. Heat just until cheese melts, stirring. Spear bread with fork; dunk into fondue. 4 servings.

EGGS AND OYSTERS AU GRATIN

1 can (10 ounces) frozen condensed
   oyster stew
1 tablespoon flour
¼ cup milk or water
1 cup shredded sharp Cheddar
   cheese
2 hard-cooked eggs, sliced
1 pound asparagus or broccoli (or
   a 10-ounce package frozen),
   cooked and well drained
Dash paprika

Thaw soup over low heat; stir often. Make a smooth paste of flour and milk; pour into oyster stew. Heat, stirring constantly until thickened. Add cheese; continue to cook until cheese is melted. Fold in eggs. Pour over hot asparagus or broccoli. Garnish with paprika. 4 servings.

EGGS FLORENTINE

2 cups chopped cooked spinach (or
   two 10-ounce packages frozen),
   drained
6 eggs
1 can (10½ ounces) condensed
   cream of celery or mushroom soup
1 cup shredded mild process cheese

Cover bottom of shallow baking dish (10 x 6 x 2″) with cooked spinach; break eggs and place on top. Pour soup around eggs completely covering spinach; sprinkle with cheese. Bake in a 350° oven 25 to 30 minutes or until eggs are done. 6 servings.

QUICK EGG CURRY

1 can (10½ ounces) condensed
   cream of mushroom soup
⅓ cup milk
1 teaspoon curry powder
4 hard-cooked eggs, sliced
4 slices bread, toasted
Shredded coconut, toasted slivered
   almonds, chutney, or raisins

Stir soup until smooth. Blend in milk and curry powder. Heat; stir often. Add eggs. Serve over toast with coconut, almonds, chutney, or raisins. 4 servings.

WESTERN SCRAMBLE

½ cup chopped cooked ham
¼ cup chopped green pepper
¼ cup chopped onion
¼ cup butter or margarine
1 can (11 ounces) condensed
   Cheddar cheese soup
8 eggs, slightly beaten

Cook ham, green pepper, and onion in butter until vegetables are tender. Stir soup until smooth; blend in eggs; add to ham mixture. Cook over low heat until eggs are set, lifting eggs gently now and then. 6 servings.

cheese soup or pkg cheese sauce

EGGS IN CHEESE SAUCE

1 can (10½ ounces) condensed
   cream of vegetable, celery,
   or mushroom soup
⅓ to ½ cup milk
½ cup shredded sharp Cheddar
   cheese
4 hard-cooked eggs, sliced
4 slices toast
Chopped parsley, if desired

Combine soup, milk, and cheese. Cook over low heat until cheese melts. Stir often. Add eggs. Serve on toast, rice, or asparagus. Garnish with parsley. 4 servings.

CURRIED EGGS AND SHRIMP

6 hard-cooked eggs
¼ cup mayonnaise
¼ teaspoon curry powder
1 can (10 ounces) frozen condensed
   cream of shrimp soup
½ soup can milk
Toast (or English muffins, split and
   toasted)
Paprika

Cut eggs in half lengthwise. Scoop out and mash yolks; stir in mayonnaise and curry powder. Refill egg halves. Combine soup and milk. Heat until soup is thawed; stir often. Place eggs, filled side up, in soup. Cover; simmer until eggs are hot. If desired, spoon soup over eggs once or twice while cooking. Place 3 egg halves on each piece of toast or English muffin. Pour soup over. Sprinkle with paprika. 4 servings.

GOLDEN RABBIT

1 can (11 ounces) condensed
   Cheddar cheese soup
1 can (10½ ounces) condensed
   tomato soup
¼ cup milk
6 slices toast or crackers

Stir cheese soup until smooth. Gradually blend in tomato soup and milk. Heat; stir often. Serve over toast or crackers. 4 to 6 servings.

Salads and Salad Dressings

Do you yearn for a special blend of seasonings to give your salads a special lift? Does your husband admire a hearty potato salad of robust flavor? Are you looking for a colorful molded salad to serve at luncheon; for smooth yet not-too-rich dressings, to set off a bowl of greens? You'll find your answer here; each flavored with that secret ingredient, a can of condensed soup.

HAM AND MACARONI TOSS

1 can (10½ ounces) condensed
    cream of chicken soup
¼ cup chopped celery
¼ cup chopped onion
2 tablespoons chopped green
    pepper
½ teaspoon prepared mustard
Dash "Tabasco" sauce
Dash pepper
2 cups cooked macaroni
1 cup diced cooked ham
Tomatoes, cut in wedges

Combine soup, celery, onion, green pepper, mustard, "Tabasco" sauce, and pepper. Add macaroni and ham. Chill. Serve with tomato wedges. 4 to 6 servings.

TIP: To unmold gelatine salads, dip pan bottom briefly in warm (not hot) water. Run knife along edges to permit air to flow in. Tap sharply once or twice. Invert on moistened serving plate (this permits you to shift mold if necessary); raise pan and release salad.

SEASHORE SALAD

2 envelopes unflavored gelatine
2 cups cold water
1 can (10¾ ounces) condensed tomato soup
1 tablespoon lemon juice
1 package (8 ounces) cream cheese, softened
1 cup diced cooked shrimp
½ cup chopped celery
2 tablespoons chopped green onion

In saucepan, sprinkle gelatine on cold water to soften. Place over low heat, stirring until gelatine is dissolved. Remove from heat; gradually stir in soup and lemon juice. Stir cream cheese until smooth; gradually blend in gelatine mixture. Chill until slightly thickened. Fold in remaining ingredients. Pour into 1-quart mold. Chill until firm. Unmold and serve on crisp salad greens. 4 servings.

CREAMY TUNA MOLD

Lemon jello

2 envelopes unflavored gelatine
2 cups cold water
1 can (10½ ounces) condensed cream of celery soup
1 tablespoon lemon juice
1 package (3 ounces) cream cheese, softened
1 can (7 ounces) tuna, drained and flaked
½ cup shredded carrot
½ cup chopped celery
2 tablespoons chopped parsley

Blender

In saucepan, sprinkle gelatine on 1 cup cold water to soften. Place over low heat, stirring until gelatine is dissolved. Remove from heat. Blend soup and lemon juice into cream cheese; gradually blend in gelatine and remaining water. Chill until slightly thickened. Fold in remaining ingredients. Pour into 5-cup mold. Chill until firm. Unmold; serve on crisp salad greens. 4 servings.

ROSY AND WHITE ASPIC

1 envelope unflavored gelatine
½ cup cold water
1 can (10½ ounces) condensed tomato soup
1 teaspoon grated onion
Crisp salad greens
1 cup creamy cottage cheese

Sprinkle gelatine on cold water to soften. Place over low heat; stir until gelatine is dissolved. Remove from heat; combine with soup and onion. Pour into 1-quart or 4 individual molds that have been rinsed with cold water. Chill until firm. Unmold; serve on salad greens with a topping of cottage cheese. 4 servings.

DOUBLE DECKER CHICKEN MOLD

First layer:
1 envelope unflavored gelatine
½ cup cold water
1 can (10½ ounces) condensed
  cream of chicken soup
¼ cup mayonnaise
1 tablespoon lemon juice
1 can (5 ounces) boned chicken,
  or 1 cup diced cooked chicken
¼ cup chopped celery
2 tablespoons chopped toasted
  almonds
1 tablespoon finely chopped onion
Dash pepper

First layer: Sprinkle gelatine on cold water to soften. Place over low heat; stir until gelatine is dissolved. Remove from heat. Blend soup, mayonnaise, and lemon juice; stir in gelatine. Chill until mixture begins to thicken. Fold in remaining ingredients. Pour into 1½-quart mold. Chill until almost firm.

Second layer:
1 envelope unflavored gelatine
½ cup cold water
1 can (1 pound) jellied cranberry
  sauce
1 orange, peeled and diced

Second layer: Sprinkle gelatine on cold water to soften. Place over low heat; stir until gelatine is dissolved. Remove from heat. Crush cranberry sauce with fork; add gelatine. Chill until mixture begins to thicken; fold in orange. Pour on top of chicken layer. Chill until firm. Unmold. Serve on crisp salad greens. 6 to 8 servings.

SPRINGTIME SALAD

Lemon jello
2 envelopes ~~unflavored gelatine~~
1 cup cold water
2 cans (10½ ounces each) condensed
  beef broth
~~1 tablespoon vinegar~~
2 drops "Tabasco" sauce
½ cup shredded carrot
½ cup sliced celery
2 tablespoons chopped pimiento
½ cup chopped fresh spinach
2 tablespoons chopped green onion

Blender

In saucepan, sprinkle gelatine on cold water to soften. Place over low heat, stirring until gelatine is dissolved. Remove from heat; add soup, vinegar, and "Tabasco" sauce. Divide into 3 portions; fold carrots into one portion. Pour into loaf pan (8x4½x2½"); chill until set but not firm. Fold celery and pimiento into second portion; spoon on carrot layer. Chill until set but not firm. Fold spinach and onion into remaining gelatine; spoon on celery layer. Chill until firm, about 3 hours. 4 to 6 servings.

GERMAN POTATO SALAD

4 slices bacon
¾ cup chopped onion
1 can (10½ ounces) condensed
  cream of celery or chicken soup
¼ cup water
2 to 3 tablespoons vinegar
½ teaspoon sugar
⅛ teaspoon pepper
4 cups sliced cooked potatoes
¼ cup chopped parsley

Cook bacon until crisp; remove from skillet; drain and crumble. Cook onion in bacon drippings until tender. Blend in soup, water, vinegar, sugar, and pepper. Heat; stir now and then. Add potatoes, parsley, and bacon; simmer 5 minutes. Serve hot. 6 servings.

TOMATO FRENCH DRESSING

1 can (10½ ounces) condensed
  tomato soup
½ soup can vinegar (½ cup plus
  2 tablespoons)
½ soup can salad oil (½ cup plus
  2 tablespoons)
2 tablespoons minced onion
2 tablespoons sugar
2 teaspoons dry mustard
1 teaspoon salt
¼ teaspoon pepper

Combine all ingredients in 1-quart jar. Shake well before using. About 2⅔ cups.

NOTE: To vary this TOMATO FRENCH DRESSING, add any one of the following:

Bacon Dressing—4 slices bacon, cooked and crumbled
Blue Cheese Dressing—¼ cup crumbled blue cheese
Chiffonade Dressing—1 chopped hard-cooked egg, 1 tablespoon minced
  green pepper, 1 tablespoon minced pimiento
Curry Dressing—½ teaspoon curry powder
Garlic Dressing—1 clove garlic, minced
Herb Dressing—1 teaspoon ground herb (marjoram, rosemary, sage,
  savory, or thyme)
Ripe Olive Dressing—¼ cup chopped ripe olives
Sweet Pickle Relish Dressing—¼ cup sweet pickle relish
Vinaigrette Dressing—1 chopped hard-cooked egg and 1 tablespoon
  chopped parsley

RUSSIAN–STYLE DRESSING

1 can (10½ ounces) condensed
  cream of celery soup
¼ cup mayonnaise
¼ cup chili sauce
1 teaspoon lemon juice
2 to 3 teaspoons minced onion,
  if desired

Place unopened can of soup in refrigerator 3 to 4 hours. Blend soup and mayonnaise; stir in remaining ingredients. Serve with asparagus or green salads. About 1¾ cups dressing.

QUICK GREEN GODDESS DRESSING

1 can (10½ ounces) condensed
  cream of celery soup
¼ cup mayonnaise
2 tablespoons chopped parsley
4 anchovies, chopped
1 teaspoon lemon juice

*½ C sour cream
onion*

Place unopened can of soup in refrigerator 3 to 4 hours. Blend soup and mayonnaise; stir in remaining ingredients. Serve with green salads. About 1½ cups dressing.

DRESSING LAMAZE

1 can (10½ ounces) condensed
  tomato soup
1 cup mayonnaise
¼ cup India or sweet pickle relish
1 hard-cooked egg, chopped
½ teaspoon grated onion
½ teaspoon prepared mustard
1 tablespoon lemon juice

Blend soup and mayonnaise. Add remaining ingredients; mix well. Chill. Serve with cooked shrimp or green salads. About 2½ cups dressing.

LOW-CAL TOMATO DRESSING

Blender

1 cup cottage cheese
1 can (10½ ounces) condensed
  tomato soup
1 tablespoon India or sweet pickle
  relish
1 tablespoon lemon juice
Grated lemon rind, if desired

Blend all ingredients; chill. Stir well and serve over green salads. About 2 cups dressing.

DIETERS' DELIGHT

1 can (10½ ounces) condensed beef
  broth
2 tablespoons chili sauce or ketchup
2 tablespoons ~~vinegar~~ *lemon or lime*
1 tablespoon grated onion
1 ounce crumbled blue cheese, if
  desired

Combine all ingredients. Shake well and serve over green salads. About 1¼ cups dressing.

Quick Breads and Pancakes

If you're looking for something new that's quick to get ready, with family-satisfying flavor, here's the formula: Prepare a stack of pancakes, or bake a quick corn bread (a mix does fine). Combine a creamy soup with chicken or ham or any of the combinations in recipes given here. Spoon the mixture over the hot bread, and you have a dish to do you proud.

Try a quick spoon bread with extra flavor baked right in the batter—soup does it!

MINUTE TURKEY SHORTCAKE

1 can (10½ ounces) condensed
   cream of chicken soup
¼ cup milk
1 cup diced cooked turkey
½ cup cooked peas
1 tablespoon chopped pimiento
4 biscuits, split

Blend soup and milk. Combine remaining ingredients except biscuits. Heat; stir often. Serve over biscuits. 4 servings.

SPOONBREAD

1 cup corn meal
1¼ cups water
3 tablespoons butter or margarine
1 can (10¾ ounces) condensed
   Cheddar cheese, cream of chicken,
   or mushroom soup
1 teaspoon baking powder
3 eggs, separated

In saucepan, combine corn meal and water; bring to a boil and cook until very thick, stirring constantly. Remove from heat and stir in butter. Add soup, baking powder, and slightly beaten egg yolks; mix well. Fold mixture into stiffly beaten egg whites. Pour into greased 2-quart casserole dish. Bake at 350°F. for 1 hour. Serve hot with butter and maple syrup if desired. 6 servings.

PANCAKES

Most recipes in this section call for 8 pancakes. You will find that your favorite pancake recipe, when made with 1 cup flour or 1 cup pancake mix, yields 7 to 8 average size pancakes.

CREAMED CHICKEN WITH ALMONDS OVER PANCAKES

1 cup chopped celery
2 tablespoons butter or margarine
1 can (10½ ounces) condensed cream of chicken or mushroom soup
⅓ to ½ cup milk
1 can (5 ounces) boned chicken, or 1 cup diced cooked chicken
2 tablespoons diced pimiento
¼ cup toasted slivered almonds, if desired
Pancakes

Cook celery in butter until tender; blend in soup and milk. Add chicken, pimiento, and almonds. Heat; stir often. Serve over pancakes. 4 servings.

HAM-AND-MUSHROOM-STUFFED PANCAKES

8 thin pancakes (about 7 inches in diameter)
1 can (2 ounces) mushroom stems and pieces, drained and chopped
2 tablespoons finely chopped onion
2 tablespoons butter or margarine
8 thin slices boiled ham
1 can (10½ ounces) condensed cream of celery soup
½ cup sour cream
⅓ cup water
Paprika or chopped parsley

Prepare pancakes (use 1 cup pancake mix; prepare as directed on label; set aside). In saucepan, cook mushrooms and onion in butter until onion is tender. Place a slice of ham and 2 teaspoons mushroom mixture on each pancake; roll. Keep warm in oven. Meanwhile, combine soup, sour cream, and water. Heat; stir now and then. Serve sauce over pancakes. Garnish with paprika or chopped parsley. 4 servings. (2 pancakes per serving)

CHINESE SHRIMP PANCAKES

8 thin pancakes (about 7 inches in diameter)
¼ cup sliced water chestnuts
2 tablespoons thinly sliced green onion
2 tablespoons butter or margarine
1 can (10 ounces) frozen condensed cream of shrimp soup, thawed
1 cup diced cooked shrimp
¼ teaspoon soy sauce
2 tablespoons milk
¼ teaspoon Worcestershire
Dash "Tabasco" sauce

Prepare pancakes; set aside. Cook water chestnuts and onion in butter a few minutes. Add ¼ cup of soup, shrimp, and soy sauce. Place 2 tablespoons of filling on each pancake; roll. Keep warm in oven. Combine remaining soup, milk, Worcestershire, and "Tabasco" sauce. Heat. Serve as sauce over pancakes. 4 servings.

Surprise Cakes and Cookies

Tomato soup gives a wonder-what-it-is flavor and rosy color to cakes and cookies.

Once tried, these are the unusual cake specialties you will want to make again and again. Some women win blue ribbons at fairs with tomato soup cakes; others bake them for holiday gifts. Most women make them just for the pleasure of baking an easy cake with fascinating flavor—a little spicy, a little tangy, and altogether special.

Cake mix users will find that spicy cakes made with tomato soup have more than extra flavor.

ROSY CHIFFON CAKE

2¼ cups sifted cake flour
1½ cups sugar
3 teaspoons baking powder
1 teaspoon baking soda
1½ teaspoons allspice
1 teaspoon ground cinnamon
½ teaspoon ground cloves
1 can (10¾ ounces) condensed tomato soup
½ cup salad oil
¼ cup water
5 egg yolks
1 cup egg whites (7 to 8)
½ teaspoon cream of tartar

Preheat oven to 325°F. Sift together flour, sugar, baking powder, soda, and spices into mixing bowl. Make a well in flour mixture; add soup, oil, water, and egg yolks; beat until smooth. Beat egg whites and cream of tartar together in large mixing bowl until they form *very stiff* peaks. Pour egg yolk mixture gradually over whites, gently folding with rubber spatula until completely blended. Pour into ungreased 10-inch tube pan. Bake at 325°F. for 65 to 70 minutes or until top springs back when lightly touched. Remove from oven and turn pan upside down over neck of funnel; let cool at least 1 hour. Loosen cake around edge and tube of pan with spatula; remove from pan and glaze if desired.

GLAZE FOR ROSY CHIFFON CAKE

3 tablespoons milk
2 tablespoons butter or margarine
2 cups sifted confectioners' sugar
2 teaspoons grated lemon rind
2 teaspoons lemon juice

In saucepan, heat milk with butter. Stir into sugar, beating until smooth. Blend in rind and juice. Makes ⅔ cup glaze; enough for 10-inch tube cake.

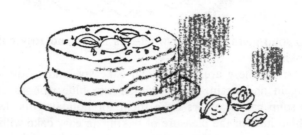

TOMATO SOUP CAKE

2¼ cups sifted cake flour or 2 cups sifted all-purpose flour
1⅓ cups sugar
4 teaspoons baking powder
1 teaspoon baking soda
1½ teaspoons allspice
1 teaspoon cinnamon
½ teaspoon ground cloves
½ cup hydrogenated shortening
1 can (10¾ ounces) condensed tomato soup
2 eggs
¼ cup water

Preheat oven to 350°F. Grease and flour two round layer pans, 8 or 9 x 1½" or an oblong pan, 13 x 9 x 2". Sift dry ingredients together into large bowl. Add shortening and soup. Beat at low to medium speed for 2 minutes (300 strokes with a spoon) scraping sides and bottom of bowl constantly. Add eggs and water. Beat 2 minutes more, scraping bowl frequently. Pour into pans. Bake 25 to 30 minutes. Let stand in pans 10 minutes; remove and cool on rack. Frost with Cream Cheese Frosting.

VARIATIONS: For a 9-inch tube pan. Prepare as above; bake 1 hour.
Nut or Raisin: After mixing, fold in 1 cup chopped nuts or 1 cup raisins. Bake 35 to 40 minutes.

Date and Nut: After mixing, fold in 1 cup chopped walnuts and 1 cup chopped dates. (Use 1 to 2 tablespoons flour to sprinkle over dates while chopping them.) Bake in 9" layers or 13 x 9 x 2" pan for 40 to 45 minutes.

CREAM CHEESE FROSTING

Blend 2 packages (3 ounces each) cream cheese (softened) with 1 tablespoon milk. Gradually add 1 package (1 pound) sifted confectioners' sugar; blend well. Mix in ½ teaspoon vanilla extract, if desired.

QUICK TOMATO SPICE CAKE

1 package (2 layer) spice cake mix
1 teaspoon baking soda
1 can (10¾ ounces) condensed tomato soup
½ cup water
2 eggs

Combine ingredients. Mix and bake cake as directed on package.

EASY FRUIT CAKE

Prepare QUICK TOMATO SPICE CAKE. After mixing, fold in 1 cup chopped candied fruit and 1 cup chopped walnuts. Bake as directed on package adding about 5 minutes more.

FOR MINCEMEAT CAKE. Substitute ½ cup prepared mincemeat for candied fruit in EASY FRUIT CAKE. Bake in 9" layers or 13 x 9 x 2" pan.

APRICOT OR PRUNE UPSIDE DOWN CAKE

Divide between two 9-inch round layer pans: ½ cup melted butter, ½ cup brown sugar; top with an arrangement of 1 can (1 pound) apricot halves, drained (about 1 cup) and ½ cup walnut pieces. Prepare QUICK TOMATO SPICE CAKE. Pour into pans spreading evenly over topping. Bake at 350°F. for 35 minutes. Run spatula around edge of pan. Immediately turn upside down on serving plate. Leave pan over cake 5 minutes. Serve warm or cooled.

FOR PRUNE CAKE: Follow directions above, substituting 1 jar or can (1 pound) canned pitted prunes, drained (about 1 cup) for apricots.

FOAMY SAUCE
(For Steamed Pudding)

1 egg, separated
¾ cup confectioners' sugar
¾ cup heavy cream
½ teaspoon vanilla extract

With rotary beater, beat egg white until it stands in soft peaks; gradually beat in sugar. Stir in egg yolk. Whip cream; fold into egg mixture along with vanilla extract. 2 cups sauce.

STEAMED PUDDING

2½ cups sifted all-purpose flour
3 teaspoons baking powder
½ teaspoon baking soda
1 teaspoon ground cinnamon
½ teaspoon ground nutmeg
2 cups chopped dates or figs
¼ cup shortening
1 cup sugar
1 egg
1 can (10½ ounces) condensed tomato soup

Sift flour with baking powder, soda, and spices; dust dates or figs with small amount of flour mixture. Cream shortening and sugar; add egg and mix well. Add dry ingredients alternately with soup; stir well after each addition. Fold in dates or figs. Pour into greased 1½-quart mold; cover securely with aluminum foil. Place on trivet in large kettle. Add boiling water to one-half height of mold. Cover; steam 2 hours. Remove mold from water; uncover and loosen edges of pudding with knife. Unmold while hot; serve with one of the following sauces, Foamy Sauce or Hard Sauce.

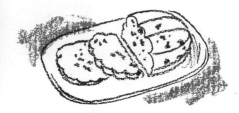

HARD SAUCE

⅓ cup soft butter
1 cup sifted confectioners' sugar
½ teaspoon vanilla extract

In bowl, soften butter. Add sugar, a little at a time; beat until creamy and smooth. Stir in vanilla extract. Chill until hard. ¾ cup sauce.

ROSY ROCKS

1½ cups all-purpose flour
1⅓ cups sugar
1 teaspoon baking powder
½ teaspoon baking soda
2 teaspoons cinnamon
1 teaspoon allspice
1 cup shortening
1 egg
1 can (10¾ ounces) condensed tomato soup
2 cups uncooked rolled oats
1 cup seedless raisins
1 cup chopped walnuts

Preheat oven to 350°F. Sift dry ingredients except oats together into large bowl. Add shortening, egg, and soup. Beat at medium speed for 2 minutes (300 strokes with a spoon), scraping sides and bottom of bowl constantly. Stir in oats, raisins, and nuts. Drop rounded teaspoonfuls on ungreased cookie sheet. Bake about 15 minutes or until lightly browned. Makes about 7 dozen cookies.

Party and International Specialties

"Let's have a party."

Happy words indeed. And they lead up to some of the most memorable occasions for every family—when good friends get together.

What kind of party? Name most any kind—and good food will be a key factor to its success: Children's birthdays. Teenage record hops. Grandparents' golden wedding anniversary. Even when the girl next door comes for coffee, it can be a party.

TODAY'S SERVICE, BUFFET STYLE

An easy style of service is a major requirement for today's parties because of smaller homes without dining rooms and little outside help. Buffet service is the answer for many a hostess. Nothing is more dazzling for guests to behold than a buffet table covered with colorful tempting foods. Each one picks up a plate and helps himself while the hostess guides the proceedings.

Successful buffets are those where guests are at ease to enjoy the company and the food. Some pointers to follow are these:

1. Plan the menu with an eye for color. If the main dish is a casserole, top it with golden cheese or some slices of tomato or stuffed olives for that bit of color.
2. Serve at least one hot dish (perhaps a vegetable). Or if you're serving mainly hot foods, include relishes or a chilled fruit dessert for contrast.
3. Plan the food so the main course and accompaniments can all go on one's dinner plate. To achieve this, it's often helpful to serve vegetable relishes and spiced fruits instead of a salad.
4. Fork foods are best because guests won't have to worry about several pieces of silverware to juggle. Plan a meat that can be cut with a fork (for example—sliced ham or boned chicken); or use a main dish such as chicken à la king which requires no cutting.
5. Trays are a necessity if guests do not sit at a table to eat.

GOOD STARTERS

The appetizer course starts a party in sparkling fashion. This is why it's becoming fashionable to serve a "cup of soup" in the living room for guests to sip and savor before the meal. Now's the time to bring forth your handsome old tureen or a lovely pitcher for a pouring soup.

Select the soup course from any of those given in the "Appetizer Soup" section. Or perhaps one of these:

FRISKY SOUR

2 cans (10½ ounces each) condensed beef broth
½ soup can water
8 ice cubes
¼ to ⅓ cup lemon juice

Put all ingredients in a shaker or jar with tight fitting cover. Cover and shake well. Serve in chilled glasses. 4 to 6 servings.

FLAMING BEAN SOUP

2 cans (10½ ounces each) condensed black bean soup
1 can (10½ ounces) condensed beef broth
2 soup cans water
¼ cup sherry or bourbon
Lemon slices

Blend soups; add water. Heat; stir often. Pour into heat-proof chafing dish or tureen. To flame, heat the sherry or bourbon in a ladle. Put a lighted match to warmed liquor. While flaming, lower into the soup. Stir to blend the flavors before ladling out this warming brew. Pass lemon slices for garnish. 6 servings.

TANGY SPLIT PEA BOWL

1 can (2 ounces) sliced mushrooms, drained
⅛ teaspoon thyme
1 tablespoon butter or margarine
1 can (11¼ ounces) condensed split pea with ham soup
1 soup can water

Lightly brown mushrooms with thyme in butter. Add soup; gradually stir in water. Heat; stir often. 2 to 3 servings.

PARTY PATTERN SOUPS

Often just a small touch of decoration for food can give a party air to a simple menu—which may be merely soup and sandwiches. For example, an easy-to-do soup garnish can be croutons cut in various shapes to make "Party Pattern Soups".

BRIDGE LUNCHEON: Cut white bread into bridge shapes (diamonds, hearts, clubs, and spades)—use small cookie cutters. Toast lightly and float one crouton on each bowl of cream soup.

Other party-pattern garnishes to try:

- Valentine's Day: Heart-shaped croutons.
- St. Patrick's Day: Shamrock-shaped croutons.
- July Fourth: Star-shaped croutons.
- Halloween: Pumpkin-shaped croutons.
- Christmas: Simple tree-shaped croutons.

SPECIALTY DISHES

"Make one great dish your specialty" is a secret to successful parties used by many a hostess. You can borrow from the great cooking of the world to make dishes with that gourmet flair. Many ideas follow.

WHEN THE GALS MEET

Chilled V-8   Sesame Seed Wafers
Lobster Fondue* or
Seafood Curry*
Mixed Green Salad
Minted Pineapple   Fancy Cookies
Tea or Coffee

LOBSTER FONDUE

1 can (10 ounces) frozen condensed
   cream of shrimp soup
½ soup can milk
½ cup shredded sharp cheese
½ cup cooked or canned lobster,
   cut-up
Dash paprika
Dash cayenne
2 tablespoons sherry (optional)

In a chafing dish or saucepan, combine soup and milk. Heat slowly until soup is thawed. Add cheese, lobster, paprika, and cayenne. Heat; stir often until cheese melts. Add sherry. Use as an appetizer dunk with large cubes of bread, or pour over toast slices spread with dill butter for a luncheon dish. 3 to 4 servings.

SEAFOOD CURRY

¼ cup chopped onion
1 to 2 teaspoons curry powder
1 tablespoon butter
1 can (10 ounces) frozen condensed
   cream of shrimp soup
⅓ to ½ cup milk
1 cup flaked cooked crab, lobster,
   or diced cooked shrimp (or one 6-
   ounce can, drained)
Cooked rice or patty shells

Cook onion and curry powder in butter until onion is tender. Add soup, milk, and crab. Heat until soup is thawed; stir often. Serve over rice or in patty shells. 4 servings.

JAMBALAYA

1½ cups diced cooked ham
2 tablespoons salad oil
1 cup chopped onion
½ cup chopped green pepper
1 clove garlic, minced
1 can (10½ ounces) condensed
   tomato soup
1½ cups water
¾ cup uncooked rice
1 bay·leaf
¼ teaspoon salt
¼ teaspoon leaf thyme, crushed
Dash pepper
1 pound shrimp, cooked and cleaned
   (or two 6-ounce cans, drained)
Chopped parsley

Lightly brown ham in oil; add onion, green pepper, and garlic. Cook until vegetables are tender. Add remaining ingredients except shrimp and parsley; bring to boil; cover. Turn heat very low. Cook 20 minutes; stir after 10 minutes. Add shrimp; remove from heat; let stand covered 10 minutes. Fluff rice with fork. Garnish with parsley. 4 to 6 servings.

A TOUCH OF PARIS

French Onion Soup* (see index)
Scallops Parisienne*
Buttered Green Peas
Endive Salad with Tomato French Dressing*
French Bread   Butter
Fruit Turnovers (from freezer)
Coffee

SCALLOPS PARISIENNE

2 tablespoons chopped onion
1 can (3 ounces) sliced mushrooms,
   drained
2 tablespoons butter or margarine
1 pound fresh scallops
1 can (10¾ ounces) condensed
   cream of vegetable soup
2 tablespoons milk
2 teaspoons lemon juice
Dash pepper
Dash leaf thyme
Dash ground marjoram
2 tablespoons buttered bread
   crumbs

Lightly brown onion and mushrooms in butter. Add scallops; cook a few minutes; pour off drippings. Place scallops in shallow baking dish (or 3 or 4 individual dishes). Combine soup, milk, lemon juice, and seasonings; pour over scallops. Top with crumbs. Bake in a 350° oven 30 minutes. 3 to 4 servings.

SHRIMP WITH NOODLES

1 can (10 ounces) frozen condensed
   cream of shrimp soup
⅓ cup water
½ cup sour cream
1 cup cooked shrimp (or one 6-
   ounce can, drained)
⅛ teaspoon paprika
2 cups cooked noodles

Heat soup and water until soup is thawed. Blend in sour cream. Add shrimp and paprika. Heat a few minutes; stir often. Serve over noodles. 4 servings.

SHRIMP AND ARTICHOKE HEARTS

1 package (10 ounces) frozen artichoke hearts, cooked and drained
1 can (4 ounces) sliced mushrooms, drained
1 tablespoon butter or margarine
1 can (10 ounces) frozen condensed cream of shrimp soup
¼ cup milk
1 tablespoon sherry (optional)
1 teaspoon Worcestershire
1 tablespoon grated Parmesan cheese
Dash paprika

Place artichoke hearts in buttered 1-quart casserole. Brown mushrooms in butter; add soup, milk, sherry, and Worcestershire. Heat until soup is thawed; stir often. Pour over artichokes. Top with cheese and paprika. Bake in a 375° oven 20 minutes. Ideal for buffet. 3 to 4 servings.

SUPPER ITALIANO

Antipasto Tray
Chicken Cacciatore with Spaghetti*
Romaine Salad
Bread Sticks
Fruit   Cheese
Caffè Espresso

CHICKEN CACCIATORE

2 pounds chicken parts
2 tablespoons shortening
1 can (10¾ ounces) condensed tomato soup
¼ cup water
¼ cup dry red wine or 1 tablespoon vinegar
2 large cloves garlic, minced
1 teaspoon oregano, crushed
¼ teaspoon salt
½ medium green pepper, cut into strips
½ cup chopped onion

In skillet, brown chicken in shortening; pour off fat. Add remaining ingredients. Cover; cook over low heat 45 min.; stir now and then. Uncover; cook until sauce thickens to desired consistency. 4 to 6 servings. Serve with spaghetti.

IT'S A CURRY PARTY
Supper Party Starter*
Curried Chicken with Almonds*
Parsley Rice
Chutney   Preserved Kumquats
Jellied Vegetable Salad
Coconut Cake   Coffee

CURRIED CHICKEN WITH ALMONDS

1 pound chicken breasts
3 tablespoons seasoned flour
Shortening
1 can (10½ ounces) condensed
  cream of chicken soup
½ to ¾ cup water
½ to 1 teaspoon curry powder
1 tablespoon chopped pimiento
¼ cup toasted slivered almonds

Dust chicken with seasoned flour. Brown chicken in shortening. Combine remaining ingredients except almonds; pour over chicken. Cover. Cook over low heat 40 minutes or until chicken is tender. Stir often. (Add a little more water if necessary.) Add almonds. Cover. Cook 5 minutes more. 2 to 3 servings.

CHICKEN PAPRIKA

4 pounds chicken parts
⅓ cup seasoned flour
⅓ cup shortening
2 cans (10½ ounces each) condensed
  tomato soup
½ cup water
2 cans (4 ounces each) sliced
  mushrooms, drained
½ cup chopped onion
1 tablespoon paprika
1 large bay leaf
1 cup sour cream

Dust chicken with flour; brown in shortening in large skillet. Pour off fat. Stir in remaining ingredients except sour cream. Cover; simmer 45 minutes or until tender. Stir now and then. Remove bay leaf. Blend in sour cream. Heat. Serve with noodles. 8 to 10 servings.

SOUPER MACARONI AND CHEESE

The favorite basic casserole to go with any meat dish at your buffet supper.

2 cups cooked macaroni
1 tablespoon butter or margarine
1 can (10½ ounces) condensed
  cream of mushroom soup
⅓ cup water
1 cup shredded Cheddar cheese
1 tablespoon finely minced onion

In 1½-quart casserole, blend hot cooked macaroni with butter. Stir in soup, water, ¾ cup cheese, and onion. Sprinkle remaining cheese on top. Bake in a 350° oven about 30 minutes or until browned and bubbly. 4 servings.

TOMATO MACARONI: Use ingredients and directions as above, but substitute 1 can condensed tomato soup for the cream of mushroom soup.

BREAST OF CHICKEN MAGNIFIQUE

4 whole chicken breasts (about 3 pounds), split
¼ cup butter or margarine
2 cups sliced mushrooms (about ½ pound)
2 cans (10½ ounces each) condensed cream of chicken soup
1 large clove garlic, minced
Generous dash crushed thyme
⅛ teaspoon rosemary, crushed
⅔ cup light cream

Use 1 large skillet or prepare in 2 skillets (10 inch) by dividing the ingredients equally. Brown chicken in butter; remove. Brown mushrooms. Stir in soup, garlic, and seasonings; add chicken. Cover; cook over low heat 45 minutes. Stir now and then. Blend in cream; heat slowly. Serve with rice. 8 servings.

CHICKEN VIA VENETO

4 pounds chicken parts
¼ cup flour
¼ cup butter
1 cup ham strips
2 cans (10¾ ounces each) condensed Cheddar cheese soup
1 cup chopped canned tomatoes
3 medium onions, quartered
1 teaspoon basil, crushed

Use 1 large skillet or prepare in 2 skillets (about 10 inch) by dividing ingredients equally. Dust chicken with flour; brown in butter; remove. Brown ham. Stir in soup, tomatoes, Onions, and basil; add chicken. Cover; cook over low heat 45 minutes or until tender. Stir now and then. Uncover; cook until desired consistency. 8 servings.

TOKYO TURKEY

1 medium onion, sliced
1 can (4 ounces) sliced mushrooms, drained
⅛ teaspoon ground ginger
1 tablespoon salad oil
1 can (10½ ounces) condensed cream of celery soup
⅔ cup water
1 can (5 ounces) boned turkey, or 1 cup diced cooked turkey
1 can (5 ounces) water chestnuts, drained and sliced
⅓ cup cooked chopped spinach
1 tablespoon soy sauce
Cooked rice

Cook onion, mushrooms, and ginger in oil until onion is tender. Stir in soup, water, turkey, chestnuts, spinach, and soy sauce. Cook over low heat 10 minutes; stir often. Serve over rice. 3 to 4 servings.

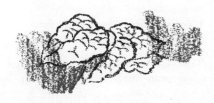

NEAR EAST MEATBALLS

1 pound ground beef
¼ cup fine dry bread crumbs
2 tablespoons milk
¼ teaspoon salt
1 can (4 ounces) sliced
  mushrooms, drained
1 tablespoon shortening
1 can (10½ ounces) condensed
  onion soup
1 cup water
½ cup uncooked rice
Minced parsley

Combine ground beef, bread crumbs, milk, and salt. Shape into 18 meatballs. Brown meatballs and mushrooms in shortening. Pour in soup and water; bring to a boil; stir in rice. Cover; simmer gently 30 minutes or until rice is tender. Stir often. Garnish with parsley. 6 servings.

QUICK LASAGNE

½ pound ground beef
1 cup chopped onion
2 large cloves garlic, minced
2 teaspoons oregano, crushed
2 cans (10¾ ozs. each) condensed
  tomato soup
½ cup water
2 teaspoons vinegar
½ pound plain lasagne
  noodles, cooked and drained
1 pint cottage cheese or ricotta
½ pound Mozzarella cheese,
  thinly sliced
Grated Parmesan cheese

In saucepan, brown beef and cook onion, garlic, oregano. Add soup, water, vinegar. Simmer 30 min.; stir now and then. In baking dish (12 x 8 x 2''), arrange 3 alternate layers of noodles, cottage cheese, meat sauce, Mozzarella. Top with Parmesan. Bake at 350°F. for 30 min. Let stand 15 min. 6 servings.

MOCK SUKIYAKI

1 pound thinly sliced round steak
2 tablespoons salad oil
1½ cups sliced celery
1 medium green pepper, sliced
1 large onion, thinly sliced
1½ cups sliced fresh mushrooms
  (or 6-ounce can, drained)
½ cup sliced green onion (1-inch
  pieces)
1 can (10½ ounces) condensed beef
  broth
1 tablespoon soy sauce
¼ cup water
2 tablespoons cornstarch
4 cups hot cooked rice

Brown meat in salad oil. Add vegetables, beef broth, and soy sauce. Cover. Cook over low heat 10 minutes or until vegetables are just tender. Stir often. Combine water and cornstarch; add to meat mixture; stir until thickened. Serve over hot rice. 4 to 6 servings.

DAD'S BIRTHDAY DINNER

Pork Chops with Party Hats*

Scalloped Potatoes* (see index)   Brussels Sprouts

Apple and Nut Salad   Muffins

Birthday Cake

Coffee   Milk

PORK CHOPS WITH PARTY HATS

4 pork chops (about 1 pound)
Dash pepper
4 onion slices
4 green pepper rings
1 can (10½ ounces) condensed
tomato soup

Brown chops on both sides in oven-proof skillet; sprinkle with pepper. Place a slice of onion and a green pepper ring on each chop; pour soup over. Cover. Bake in a 350° oven 45 minutes or until chops are tender. 4 servings.

VEAL SWISS STYLE

1½ pounds thinly sliced veal cutlet
(about ⅛-inch thick)
4 ounces sliced Swiss cheese
4 ounces sliced boiled ham
2 tablespoons flour
¼ teaspoon paprika
¼ cup butter or margarine
1 can (10½ ounces) condensed
cream of mushroom soup
⅔ cup light cream or milk
¼ cup sauterne or other dry white
wine (optional)

Cut veal into 12 oblong pieces. On each of 6 pieces, place a slice of cheese and a slice of ham. Cover with another piece of veal. Fasten securely with toothpicks. Coat lightly with flour-paprika mixture. Brown cutlets on both sides in butter. Blend remaining ingredients; pour over cutlets. Cook over low heat 30 minutes; stir often. Remove toothpicks. 6 servings.

VEAL MARSALA

1 pound veal, thinly sliced
¼ cup grated Parmesan cheese
2 tablespoons flour
Dash pepper
1 can (4 ounces) sliced mushrooms,
drained
¼ cup butter or margarine
1 can (10½ ounces) condensed
beef broth
2 tablespoons Marsala or dry red
wine (optional)
Cooked noodles or spaghetti

Cut veal into 2- or 3-inch pieces. Mix cheese, flour, and pepper; pound into veal with meat hammer or edge of heavy saucer. Brown veal, then mushrooms, in butter. Blend in any remaining flour and cheese. Add beef broth and wine. Cover. Cook over low heat 30 minutes or until meat is tender; stir often. Uncover; cook until sauce is desired consistency. Serve over noodles or spaghetti. 4 servings.

98

Shrimp Soup
Saucy Sirloin*
Hot Rice   Green Beans Amandine
Assorted Relishes
Brown 'n Serve Rolls   Butter
Apple Strudel (from freezer)
Coffee

SAUCY SIRLOIN

1 pound sirloin tip
2 tablespoons flour
Dash dry mustard
2 tablespoons butter or margarine
¼ cup chopped green onion
1 can (2 ounces) sliced mushrooms, drained
1 can (10½ ounces) condensed consomme
¼ cup dry red wine (optional)
1 teaspoon Worcestershire
Chopped parsley

Cut sirloin across the grain in slices about ⅛-inch thick; sprinkle with flour and mustard. Brown meat in butter; add onion and mushrooms; cook a few minutes longer. Stir in consomme, wine, and Worcestershire; simmer 15 minutes or until sauce is desired consistency. Stir now and then. Garnish with parsley. 4 servings. Serve with cooked rice, if desired.

CREAMED CHICKEN AND MUSHROOMS

1 can (4 ounces) sliced mushrooms, drained
¼ cup chopped onion
2 tablespoons butter or margarine
1 can (10¾ ounces) condensed cream of vegetable soup
½ cup sour cream
2 tablespoons chopped parsley
1 tablespoon sherry (optional)
½ teaspoon paprika
1 can (5 ounces) boned chicken, or 1 cup diced cooked chicken
3 cups cooked noodles

Cook mushrooms and onion in butter until tender. Stir in soup, sour cream, parsley, sherry, and paprika; add chicken. Heat; stir often. Serve over noodles. 3 to 4 servings.

2 tablespoons chopped onion
1 tablespoon butter or margarine
1 can (10½ ounces) condensed
  cream of mushroom soup
½ cup water
½ cup shredded sharp process
  cheese
1 tablespoon sherry (optional)
2 cups cooked spaghetti
1 cup diced cooked chicken
  or turkey
2 tablespoons chopped pimiento
1 tablespoon chopped parsley

Cook onion in butter until tender. Blend in soup, water, cheese, and sherry. Cook over low heat until cheese is melted; stir often. Add remaining ingredients; heat. 3 to 4 servings.

NOTE: For variety, instead of chicken in above recipe, brown 1 cup finely diced cooked ham along with onion; then prepare as directed.

GLAZED COLD MEATS

Have you ever wanted to set out a platter of cold meats for a crowd and then been disappointed to see how quickly they dry and curl? Try this simple attractive and delicious way to glaze a mixed platter of cold cuts, so that they may be arranged in advance.

1 envelope unflavored gelatine
¼ cup cold water
1 can (10½ ounces) condensed
  consomme
1 teaspoon Worcestershire
2 teaspoons lemon juice
1 can (8 ounces) pitted cherries,
  drained and rinsed in cold water
Sliced cooked ham, beef, pork,
  or lamb

Sprinkle gelatine on cold water to soften. Place over low heat; stir until gelatine is dissolved. Add consomme, Worcestershire, lemon juice, and cherries. Chill until mixture begins to thicken. Meanwhile, arrange cold meats attractively on a platter. Spoon a thin layer of the cherry consomme over meat, arranging cherries down sides and center of platter. Chill until serving time.

PARTY SALADS

A spectacular gelatine salad, shaped in a handsome mold, is a happy choice for the *pièce de résistance* for your luncheon party in the summer.

Try this menu pattern—with endless variations—to please "the girls".

FAVORITE SALAD LUNCHEON

Hot Clear Soup
Chicken or Beef Gelatine Salad
Melba Toast, Crisp Rye Wafers and Hot Rolls
Sherbet   Angel Food Cake
Coffee or Tea

HAWAIIAN CHICKEN VELVET SALAD

1 envelope unflavored gelatine
¼ cup cold water
1 can (10½ ounces) condensed
  cream of chicken soup
3 ounces cream cheese, softened
2 tablespoons lemon juice
Dash ground ginger
1 cup diced cooked chicken
½ cup drained pineapple tidbits
¼ cup chopped celery
¼ cup chopped green pepper
Crisp salad greens
Toasted slivered almonds

Sprinkle gelatine on cold water to soften. Place over low heat; stir until gelatine is dissolved. Remove from heat. Gradually blend soup into cream cheese; stir in gelatine, lemon juice, and ginger; add chicken, pineapple, celery, and green pepper. Pour into a 1-quart mold; chill until firm. Unmold; serve on crisp salad greens; garnish with toasted almonds. 6 servings.

BEEF TOMATO SALAD

2 envelopes unflavored gelatine
1½ cups water
1 bay leaf
1 can (10½ ounces) condensed
  consomme
1 can (10¾ ounces) condensed
  tomato soup
2 tablespoons vinegar
⅛ teaspoon celery salt
1 cup finely chopped cooked beef
½ cup chopped celery
¼ cup chopped cucumber
2 tablespoons chopped onion

In saucepan, sprinkle gelatine on water to soften. Add bay leaf. Place over low heat and stir until gelatine is dissolved. Remove from heat and stir in soups, vinegar, and celery salt. Remove bay leaf. Chill until mixture begins to thicken. Fold in remaining ingredients. Pour into 5½-cup mold. Chill until firm. Unmold; serve on crisp salad greens. 6 to 8 servings.

Special Occasion Meats

BEEF ITALIANO

1 boneless chuck (about 3½ pounds)
1 cup sliced onion
1 large clove garlic, minced
2 teaspoons oregano, crushed
3 tablespoons butter or margarine
1 can (10¾ ounces) condensed
   tomato soup
1 cup water
Generous dash pepper

Trim fat from meat; place in roasting pan. Bake at 350°F. for 1½ hours. Spoon off fat. Meanwhile, in saucepan, cook onion, garlic, and oregano in butter until onion is tender. Stir in remaining ingredients. Pour over meat. Cover; bake 1½ hours more or until tender. Thicken sauce if desired. 6 servings.

STEWED CHICKEN WITH DUMPLINGS

2 pounds chicken parts
1 can (10½ ounces) condensed
   cream of chicken soup
1 cup water
4 small carrots, cut in 2-inch pieces
2 large stalks celery, cut in 2-inch
   pieces
1 medium onion, thickly sliced
Dash pepper
1 cup packaged biscuit mix
⅓ cup milk

Put chicken, soup, water, vegetables, and pepper in large heavy pot. Cover; simmer 40 minutes or until chicken is tender. Combine biscuit mix and milk; stir lightly with a fork. Drop dough by spoonsful onto pieces of chicken. Cook, uncovered, 10 minutes. Cover; cook 10 minutes more. 4 to 6 servings.

ROSY HAM LOAF-HORSERADISH SAUCE

1 can (10½ ounces) condensed
   tomato soup
1 pound ground lean ham
½ pound ground lean pork
½ cup fine dry bread crumbs
⅓ cup minced onion
¼ cup finely chopped celery
1 egg, slightly beaten
½ teaspoon dry mustard
Dash pepper
2 teaspoons prepared horseradish

Measure ½ cup soup; mix *thoroughly* with ham, pork, crumbs, onion, celery, egg, mustard, and pepper. Shape *firmly* into loaf; place in shallow baking pan. Bake in a 350° oven about 1¼ hours. For sauce, blend remaining soup with horseradish; heat. Serve over loaf. 6 servings.

CREAMY VEAL

1½ pounds thinly sliced veal, cut in
   serving-size pieces
1 medium onion, sliced
1 clove garlic, minced
2 tablespoons butter or margarine
1 can (10¾ ounces) condensed
   cream of vegetable soup
¼ cup water
2 to 3 teaspoons lemon juice
1 tablespoon red wine (optional)
½ teaspoon paprika
Dash pepper
1 tablespoon chopped pimiento

Brown veal, onion, and garlic in butter. Combine remaining ingredients except pimiento; pour over veal. Cover. Cook over low heat 45 minutes; stir often. Just before serving, add chopped pimiento. 6 servings.

PORK GOULASH WITH NOODLES

¼ cup flour
½ teaspoon garlic salt
Dash pepper
1½ pounds lean pork cubes
2 tablespoons shortening
1 can (10½ ounces) condensed
   onion soup
½ cup water
1 cup cooked tomatoes
½ medium green pepper, cut into
   strips
¼ cup chopped celery
⅛ teaspoon ground thyme
2 cups cooked noodles (about 4
   ounces uncooked)

Combine flour, garlic salt, and pepper; roll meat in this mixture. In skillet, brown meat in shortening; pour off any excess drippings. Add soup, water, tomatoes, green pepper, celery, and thyme. Sprinkle remaining flour over mixture. Cover; simmer 1 hour or until meat is tender; stir often. Uncover; cook 15 minutes more to thicken sauce. Serve over noodles. 6 servings.

MARDI GRAS CHICKEN LIVERS

1 package (8 ounces) frozen chicken
   livers, thawed
½ cup thinly sliced onion
⅓ cup thinly sliced celery
2 tablespoons butter or margarine
1 can (10½ ounces) condensed
   tomato soup
¼ cup chopped parsley
¼ cup water
¼ teaspoon lemon juice
Cooked rice

Cook livers, onion, and celery in butter in covered skillet until tender. Add soup, parsley, water, and lemon juice. Heat; stir now and then. Serve on rice. 3 to 4 servings.

Cooking for a Crowd

Every so often you're called on to cook for a crowd—perhaps for a church supper or a P.T.A. fund raising.

It's easy to come up with large-scale dishes and serve them with ease if you plan on cook-ahead foods readily prepared in quantity. Soup makes an ideal first course, served from mugs or plates. Soup can contribute behind the scenes, too, in making "seconds—please" main dishes and tasty vegetables to serve a crowd happily, as in these recipes designed for 16 or 20 or more portions.

FLEET'S-IN CHOWDER

2 cups water
1½ teaspoons leaf thyme
¼ teaspoon garlic powder
3 medium bay leaves
8 cans (10½ ounces each)
   condensed clam chowder
   (Manhattan style)
6 soup cans water
2 cups flaked cooked white fish
¼ cup chopped parsley

Combine 2 cups water, thyme, garlic, and bay leaves. Cover; simmer 20 minutes; remove bay leaves. Add remaining ingredients. Heat; stir now and then. 20 servings, 1 cup each.

HARVEST SOUP

3 cans (10½ ounces each) condensed
   cream of chicken soup
3 cans (10½ ounces each) condensed
   tomato soup
8 soup cans water
3 cans (10½ ounces each) condensed
   chicken gumbo soup

Combine cream of chicken soup and tomato soup; stir until smooth. Blend in water and chicken gumbo soup. Heat. 20 servings, 1 cup each.

CLUB COCKTAIL

6 cans (10½ ounces each) condensed
tomato soup
5 cans (10½ ounces each) condensed
beef broth
5 soup cans cold water
2 teaspoons Worcestershire
Dash "Tabasco" sauce

Place cans of soup in refrigerator 3 to 4 hours to chill. Blend soups and water; stir in Worcestershire and "Tabasco" sauce. Serve in chilled bowls or cups. 20 servings, 1 cup each.

FAR EASTERN CHICKEN POT

8 cans (10½ ounces each) condensed
cream of chicken soup
8 soup cans milk
¾ cup finely chopped blanched
almonds
2 tablespoons chopped parsley
⅛ teaspoon ground cloves
¼ teaspoon ground nutmeg
6 drops "Tabasco" sauce

Blend soup and milk until smooth; add remaining ingredients. Heat; *do not boil*. 20 servings, 1 cup each.

FAVORITE BEAN SOUP

7 cans (11¼ ounces each)
condensed bean with bacon soup
7 soup cans water
2 cans (1 pound each) tomatoes
2 cups cooked lima beans, drained
2 tablespoons Worcestershire

Blend soup and water. Add remaining ingredients; cook over low heat 20 minutes. 20 servings, 1 cup each.

CHICKEN A LA KING

½ cup diced green pepper
¼ cup butter or margarine
6 cans (10½ ounces each)
condensed cream of chicken soup
2 to 3 cups milk
1½ quarts diced cooked chicken
¼ cup chopped pimiento
⅛ teaspoon pepper
Toast or patty shells

In large pan, cook green pepper in butter until tender. Gradually blend in soup and milk; stir until smooth. Add chicken, pimiento, and pepper. Heat slowly; stir now and then. Serve on toast or in patty shells. 20 servings. (⅔ cup /serving)

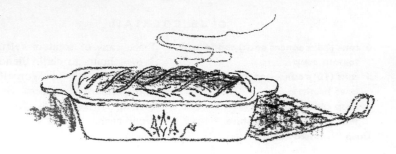

PARTY-SIZE GREEN BEAN CASSEROLE

3 cans (10½ ounces each) condensed
cream of mushroom soup
½ cup milk
1 tablespoon soy sauce
¼ teaspoon pepper
9 cups cooked French style green
beans (or six 9-ounce packages
frozen, or six 1-pound cans,
drained)
3 cans (3½ ounces each) French
fried onions

Combine soup, milk, soy sauce, and pepper; stir until smooth. Mix in beans, 1½ cans onions. Spoon into two 1½-quart casseroles. Bake in a 350° oven 30 minutes or until bubbling. Top with remaining onions. Bake 5 minutes more. 20 servings, ½ cup each.

BAKED TUNA 'N NOODLES

2 cups thinly sliced celery
½ cup chopped onion
¼ cup shortening
6 cans (10½ ounces each) condensed
cream of celery or mushroom soup
3 cups milk
6 cups cooked medium noodles
6 cans (7 ounces each) tuna, drained
and flaked
½ cup diced pimiento
½ cup buttered bread crumbs

Cook celery and onion in shortening until tender. Blend in soup and milk. Add remaining ingredients, except bread crumbs. Pour into four 1½-quart casseroles or 5 shallow baking dishes (10 x 6 x 2''). Sprinkle crumbs on top. Bake in a 375° oven 30 minutes or until bubbling and brown. 20 servings, 1 cup each. *Chicken 'N Noodles:* Substitute 6 cups diced cooked chicken for tuna. Use either cream of chicken or mushroom soup.

SOUPER HAM LOAF

2 cans (10½ ounces each) condensed
  tomato soup
2 pounds ground lean ham
2 pounds ground lean pork
2 cups fine dry bread crumbs
1 cup minced onion
½ cup chopped green pepper
3 eggs, slightly beaten
1 teaspoon dry mustard
⅛ teaspoon pepper
4 pineapple slices, cut in half

Combine soup, meats, bread crumbs, onion, green pepper, eggs, mustard, and pepper; mix *thoroughly*. Shape *firmly* into 2 loaves; place in shallow baking pan (12 x 18 x 2"). (Thorough mixing and firm shaping will result in a moist, easy-to-slice loaf.) Arrange pineapple on top. Bake in a 350° oven 1¾ hours or until done. 16 servings.

CHICKEN SUPREME

10 pounds chicken parts (40 pieces)
1 cup seasoned flour
½ cup butter or margarine, melted
6 cans (10½ ounces each) condensed
  cream of chicken or mushroom
  soup
1 cup water

Dust chicken with seasoned flour. Arrange pieces skin side down in 2 buttered baking pans (12 x 18 x 2"). Do not overlap. Dribble melted butter over chicken. Bake in a 400° oven 20 minutes. Turn chicken; bake 20 minutes longer. Blend soup and water; spread over chicken. Bake 20 minutes more or until tender. 20 servings.

BEEF ROULADES

4 pounds thinly sliced
  round steak
4 cups prepared packaged
  herb-seasoned stuffing
¼ cup shortening
2 cans (10½ ounces each) condensed
  cream of mushroom soup
1 cup water

Cut steak into 16 long pieces; pound with meat hammer or edge of heavy saucer. Place ¼ cup stuffing on each piece of steak; roll up; fasten with toothpicks. In large skillet, brown in shortening; pour off fat. Stir in soup, water. Cover; simmer 1½ hours or until tender. Stir now and then. Uncover; cook until desired consistency. 16 servings.

Teen Soups and Snacks

Fun and good food go together when teens take over the kitchen.

Soups are favorites, hot and cold, in mugs, jugs, and bowls. Add quick hot sandwiches (fast and flavorful with soup seasoning), grilled snacks, cookies—a party is set before you know it!

You'll find menus and recipes here to add to your party fun. Browse through other chapters for make-your-own party menus, from Great Soups to a Tomato Soup Cake that's "in".

AFTER-SKATING WARM-UP

Mugs of Chickety Chick*
Cheese and Crackers
Apples   Oatmeal Cookies

CHICKETY CHICK

1 can (10½ ounces) condensed
   cream of chicken soup
1 soup can water
¼ teaspoon poultry seasoning

Combine all ingredients. Heat; stir often. Sip from heavy cups or mugs. 2 to 3 servings.

VACATION SPECIAL

Watch your P's and Q's while school's out

1 can (10½ ounces) condensed
   tomato soup
1 soup can water
¼ cup cooked alphabet noodles

Blend soup and water; add noodles. Heat. 2 to 3 servings. Or for an easy switch, sprinkle alphabet cereal atop plain tomato soup.

CHILI BEEF FRANKS

¼ pound ground beef
1 can (11 ounces) condensed chili beef soup
⅓ cup water
2 teaspoons prepared mustard
1 pound frankfurters, cooked
10 frankfurter buns, slit and toasted

Brown beef; stir to separate meat particles. Add soup, water, and mustard. Heat; stir often. Place frankfurters in buns. Spoon soup mixture over. 10 servings.

CREAMY PEANUT BUTTER SOUP

1 can (10½ ounces) condensed tomato soup
¼ cup peanut butter (chunky or smooth)
1½ soup cans milk

Stir soup into peanut butter, a little at a time, until well blended; add milk. Heat, but do not boil; stir occasionally. 3 to 4 servings.

SUMMERTIME SPECIAL

Great after a swim

1 can (10½ ounces) frozen condensed green pea with ham soup
1 can (10¼ ounces) frozen condensed cream of potato soup
2 soup cans water or milk
⅛ teaspoon leaf thyme
Dash ground nutmeg, if desired

Combine all ingredients. Heat until soups are thawed. Stir often. Chill about 4 hours. Thin to desired consistency. Serve in chilled bowls with crisp carrot and cucumber sticks. 4 to 6 servings.
NOTE: May be served hot.

WINTERTIME TREAT

Warms nose and toes

1 can (2¼ ounces) deviled ham
1 teaspoon chopped parsley
3 melba rounds
¼ cup chopped onion
1 tablespoon butter or margarine
1 can (11¼ ounces) condensed green pea soup
½ soup can milk
½ soup can water

Make croutons by combining 1 tablespoon deviled ham with parsley; spread on melba rounds. Place on cookie sheet. Broil 1 to 2 minutes. Meanwhile, cook onion in butter until tender. Blend in soup, milk, water, and remaining ham. Heat; stir often. Pour soup into bowls; top each with a crouton. 3 servings.

SLOPPY JOSÉS
South of the border sloppy Joes!

1 pound ground beef
1 cup chopped onion
1 cup chopped celery
1 teaspoon chili powder
½ teaspoon salt
Dash pepper
1 tablespoon shortening
1 can (10½ ounces) condensed tomato soup
6 buns, split and toasted

Brown beef with onion, celery, and seasonings in shortening; stir to separate meat particles. Add soup; simmer to blend flavors. Serve on buns. 6 servings. A yummy supper served with crisp salads.

HOME-FROM-THE-GAME SUPPER

Frankburgers*
Celery and Carrot Sticks   Pickles
Milk
Fresh Fruit   Pretzels

FRANKBURGERS

1 can (10¾ ounces) condensed tomato soup
1½ pounds ground beef
1 teaspoon salt
⅛ teaspoon pepper
1½ teaspoons chili powder
6 frankfurter buns, split and toasted
6 frankfurters, split lengthwise
½ cup chopped onion
2 tablespoons chopped green pepper
2 tablespoons butter or margarine
1 tablespoon brown sugar
1 teaspoon vinegar

Combine ⅓ cup soup, beef, salt, pepper, and 1 teaspoon chili powder; mix thoroughly. Spread meat mixture evenly over buns; *cover edges completely.* Firmly press 2 frankfurter halves, cut side up, into the center of each bun half. Bake on broiler pan at 450°F. for 12-15 minutes. Meanwhile, in saucepan, cook onion and green pepper with remaining chili powder in butter until tender. Stir in remaining soup, sugar, and vinegar. Heat; stir now and then. Serve over sandwiches. Makes 6 open-face sandwiches.

Pizza Doggies*
Raw Vegetable Tray
Doughnuts
Cream Soda Shake

PIZZA DOGGIES

1 large clove garlic, minced
2 tablespoons olive oil
1 can (10½ ounces) condensed
  tomato soup
¼ cup water
2 tablespoons chopped parsley
¼ to ½ teaspoon leaf oregano,
  crushed
8 frankfurters, slit lengthwise
8 frankfurter buns, slit
6 ounces sliced Mozzarella cheese

Cook garlic in olive oil until lightly browned. Add soup, water, parsley, and oregano; cook over low heat 15 minutes. Stir often. Place frankfurters on buns in large shallow baking pan. Fill franks with sauce; top with cheese. Place under broiler about 1 minute or until cheese melts. 8 servings.

PRONTO CHILI

1 can (11 ounces) condensed chili
  beef soup
½ soup can water

Empty soup into saucepan; gradually blend in water. Heat; stir often. 2 servings.

BACON-TOMATO BROIL

Midnight snack for hungry dates

4 slices toast, buttered
8 slices tomato
8 slices bacon, cooked
1 can (10½ ounces) condensed
  cream of mushroom soup
⅓ cup milk
1 teaspoon finely minced onion
½ teaspoon Worcestershire

Place toast slices on cookie sheet or in shallow baking pan; top with tomato and bacon. Stir soup until smooth. Add remaining ingredients; spoon over open-face sandwiches. Broil until bubbly. 4 servings.

Chilled Cranberry Juice
Special Chicken Stack*
Fresh Fruit Cup
Rosy Rocks*
Milk and Coffee

SPECIAL CHICKEN STACK

¼ cup chopped onion
2 tablespoons butter or margarine
1 can (10½ ounces) condensed
cream of chicken soup
⅓ cup milk
1 can (5 ounces) boned chicken, or
1 cup diced cooked chicken
2 hard-cooked eggs, sliced
4 slices buttered toast
1 package (9 ounces) frozen French
style green beans, cooked

Cook onion in butter until soft but not browned; blend in soup, milk, chicken, and eggs (save several egg slices for garnish). Heat; stir often. Arrange toast on a platter; place a mound of hot beans on each slice; spoon chicken mixture over all. Garnish with egg slices. 4 servings.

BEAN 'N CORNED BEEF SPREAD

1 can (11¼ ounces) condensed
bean with bacon soup
1 cup chopped cooked corned beef
⅓ cup water
1 teaspoon prepared horseradish
1 teaspoon prepared mustard

Combine all ingredients. Spread on crunchy buttered rolls. Makes about 2 cups.

PERRITOS CON CHILE

For starving he-men

½ pound frankfurters, cut in
½-inch slices
½ cup chopped onion
2 tablespoons chopped green
pepper
½ teaspoon chili powder
2 tablespoons butter or margarine
2 cans (1 pound 4 ounces each)
kidney beans, drained
1 can (10½ ounces) condensed
tomato soup
1 teaspoon vinegar
½ teaspoon Worcestershire

Cook frankfurters, onion, green pepper, and chili powder in butter until franks are browned. Add remaining ingredients. Cover; cook over low heat 12 to 15 minutes. Stir often. 6 servings. Serve with crunchy Italian bread, cheese, and a crisp salad.

Bean 'n Bacon Burgers*
All the Trimmings
Potato Chips
Assorted Soft Drinks
Packaged Oatmeal Cookies

BEAN 'N BACON BURGERS

¼ cup chopped onion
2 tablespoons chopped green
pepper
1 tablespoon butter or margarine
1 pound ground beef
1 can (11¼ ounces) condensed
bean with bacon soup
½ cup water
⅓ cup ketchup
6 hamburger buns, toasted and
buttered

Cook onion and green pepper in butter until tender. Add beef; brown; stir to separate meat particles. Add soup, water, and ketchup; simmer about 5 minutes to blend flavors. Stir often. (Thin to desired consistency with additional water.) Serve on buns. 6 servings.

MEXICALI SUPPER

2 slices bacon
¼ cup green pepper, cut into 1-inch
strips
1 can (11 ounces) condensed chili
beef soup
½ soup can water
⅓ cup shredded mild process cheese

Cook bacon until crisp. Remove; drain and crumble. Pour off all but 1 tablespoon drippings; add green pepper and cook until tender. Stir in soup; gradually blend in water. Add cheese. Heat until cheese melts; stir often. Top with bacon. 2 servings.

SUNBATHERS' SPECIAL

Enjoy while you soak up the sun

1 can (10½ ounces) condensed
beef broth
½ soup can apple juice
Dash ground cinnamon or nutmeg,
if desired

Mix ingredients and pour over ice cubes, or heat and serve hot. 2 to 3 servings.

Sandwiches—Hot and Heroic

The sandwich has come a long way since the Earl of Sandwich asked for a slice of meat between two slices of bread, to be served at the game table. Now your favorite sandwich may make a hot and hearty lunch dish, a light supper, or an evening snack that's truly satisfying.

Have it toasted and bubbling from the grill, or with an enticing filling spooned on. The news is in your choice of sandwich filling blended with a canned soup to make a feast-on-bread.

BROILED EGG SALAD SANDWICH

1 can (10½ ounces) condensed
  cream of mushroom soup
4 hard-cooked eggs, chopped
½ cup finely chopped celery
2 tablespoons finely chopped onion
1 tablespoon sweet pickle relish
1 teaspoon prepared mustard
Dash pepper
4 frankfurter buns, split and toasted

Combine soup, eggs, celery, onion, relish, mustard, and pepper. Spread mixture evenly over bun halves; *cover edges completely.* Broil about 4 inches from heat until hot, about 7 minutes. 4 open-face sandwiches.

TOMATO, CHEESE 'N BACON BROIL

8 slices bacon, cut in half
8 slices process cheese
8 slices toast
1 can (10½ ounces) condensed
  tomato soup

Partially cook bacon. Place a slice of cheese on each slice of toast; spread with soup; *cover edges completely.* Top with bacon. Broil about 4 inches from heat until cheese melts. 8 open-face sandwiches.

TUNABURGERS

4 slices toast or toasted buns, buttered
1 can (7 ounces) tuna, drained and flaked
4 slices onion
2 hard-cooked eggs, sliced
1 can (10½ ounces) condensed cream of celery soup
⅓ cup milk
2 tablespoons chopped parsley
2 teaspoons lemon juice

Place toast on cookie sheet or in shallow baking pan; spread with tuna; top with onion and egg. Combine remaining ingredients; pour over open-face sandwiches. Broil until hot. 4 servings.

WESTERN BURGER

½ cup chopped green pepper
¼ cup chopped onion
2 tablespoons butter or margarine
1 cup chopped cooked ham
1 can (10½ ounces) condensed cream of mushroom soup
6 eggs, slightly beaten
Dash pepper
6 buns, split and toasted

Cook green pepper and onion in butter until tender. Add ham; brown. Blend soup, eggs, and pepper; add to ham and vegetables. Cook over low heat; stir now and then until eggs are set. Serve on buns. 6 servings.

CHILIBURGER

1 pound ground beef
1 tablespoon shortening
1 can (11¼ ounces) condensed bean with bacon soup
½ cup ketchup
½ teaspoon chili powder
6 buns, split and toasted

Brown beef in shortening; stir to separate meat particles. Add soup, ketchup, and chili powder; simmer about 5 minutes to blend flavors. Stir often. (Add a little water, if desired.) Serve on buns. 6 servings.

HORSERADISH SOUPERBURGER

1 pound ground beef
1 can (10½ ounces) condensed cream of mushroom soup
½ cup sour cream
1 teaspoon prepared horseradish
¼ cup chopped green pepper or pimiento
8 buns, split and toasted

Brown beef in skillet; stir often to separate meat particles. Add soup, sour cream, horseradish, and green pepper or pimiento. Simmer about 10 minutes. Serve on buns. 8 servings.

PEPPY BURGER

1 pound ground beef
½ cup chopped onion
1 tablespoon shortening
1 can (10½ ounces) condensed chicken gumbo, pepper pot, or vegetable soup
2 tablespoons ketchup
1 tablespoon prepared mustard
Dash pepper
6 buns, split and toasted

Brown beef and onion in shortening; stir to separate meat particles. Add soup and seasonings; simmer 5 to 10 minutes to blend flavors. Stir often. Serve on buns. 6 servings. NOTE: Decrease mustard to 1 teaspoon when using pepper pot and vegetable soups.

PIZZABURGER

¼ cup chopped onion
2 tablespoons shortening
1 pound ground beef
1 can (10½ ounces) condensed tomato soup
½ cup shredded sharp cheese
⅛ teaspoon oregano
Dash pepper
8 buns, split and toasted

Brown onion in shortening. Add beef; cook until browned; stir often to separate meat particles. Add soup, cheese, oregano, and pepper. Simmer about 10 minutes. Serve on buns. 8 servings.

WESTERN STYLE SANDWICH

1 can (11 ounces) condensed chili beef soup
¼ cup water
4 slices toast
4 slices tomato
4 thin slices onion
4 thin slices mild process cheese, cut into strips

Blend soup and water. Spread on toast, *covering edges completely.* Top with tomato and onion. Broil about 4 inches from heat for 5 minutes. Top with cheese; broil until cheese melts. 4 sandwiches.

BACON AND TOMATO SANDWICH

8 slices bacon
1 can (11 ounces) condensed Cheddar cheese soup
⅓ cup milk
1 teaspoon lemon juice
Dash cayenne pepper
2 medium tomatoes, sliced
4 slices toast, buttered

Cook bacon until crisp; pour off drippings. Set aside. Stir soup into skillet. Add milk, lemon juice, and pepper; blend until smooth. Heat slowly; stir often. Meanwhile, make open-face sandwiches by placing tomato and bacon on toast; pour hot sauce over. 4 servings.

FRANK AND BEAN SANDWICH

6 frankfurter buns, split and toasted
6 frankfurters, cut in half
  lengthwise
1 can (11¼ ounces) condensed
  bean with bacon soup
⅓ cup water
¼ cup ketchup
2 tablespoons sweet pickle relish

Arrange buns on cookie sheet or in shallow baking pan; place frankfurters on top. Combine remaining ingredients; *spread over frankfurters and buns completely.* Broil until hot. 6 servings.

SHRIMP-CRAB BISQUE SANDWICHES

1 can (10 ounces) frozen condensed
  cream of shrimp soup, thawed
1 can (7 ounces) crab
2 tablespoons minced celery
2 tablespoons minced green pepper
1 tablespoon minced onion
2 tablespoons mayonnaise
Few drops lemon juice
¼ teaspoon Worcestershire
Salt and pepper
4 slices toast or rusks
Grated Parmesan cheese
⅓ cup milk

Measure out ¼ cup soup; mix with crab, celery, green pepper, onion, mayonnaise, lemon juice, and seasonings. Place toast or rusks on cookie sheet. Top with crab mixture. Sprinkle with cheese. Bake in a 425° oven 10 to 15 minutes or until hot. Combine remaining soup with milk. Heat; stir often. Serve as sauce over sandwiches. 4 servings.

PUMPERNICKEL-KRAUT FRANKS

1 can (11¼ ounces) condensed
  bean with bacon soup
4 slices pumpernickel bread, lightly
  toasted
1½ cups sauerkraut, drained
4 frankfurters, slit lengthwise
¼ cup ketchup

Spread soup on bread; cover with sauerkraut. Top each sandwich with a frankfurter; spread with ketchup. Broil until sandwiches are hot, about 8 minutes. 4 servings.

CHICKEN SPREAD-A-BURGER

1 can (10½ ounces) condensed
   cream of chicken soup
1 cup diced cooked chicken
¼ cup finely chopped celery
2 tablespoons finely chopped onion
2 tablespoons chopped pimiento
Dash pepper
4 frankfurter buns, split and
   toasted

Combine soup, chicken, celery, onion, pimiento, and pepper. Spread mixture evenly over bun halves; *cover edges completely*. Broil about 4 inches from heat until hot, about 7 minutes. 4 open-face sandwiches.

CANTONESE CHICKEN SANDWICH

½ medium onion, sliced
¼ cup sliced water chestnuts
1 tablespoon butter or margarine
1 can (10½ ounces) condensed
   cream of chicken soup
⅓ cup milk
1 tablespoon soy sauce
4 servings sliced cooked chicken
   or turkey
4 slices buttered toast

Cook onion and water chestnuts in butter until onion is just tender. Stir in soup, milk, and soy sauce. Heat; stir often. Arrange chicken on toast; pour sauce over. 4 servings.

CHINA BOY SANDWICH

1 can (10½ ounces) condensed
   cream of mushroom soup
1 cup diced cooked chicken
¼ cup thinly sliced celery
¼ cup sliced water chestnuts
¼ cup chopped onion
1 teaspoon soy sauce
4 frankfurter buns, split and toasted

Combine soup, chicken, celery, water chestnuts, onion, and soy sauce. Spread mixture evenly over bun halves; *cover edges completely*. Broil about 4 inches from heat until hot, about 7 minutes. 4 open-face sandwiches.

SAUCY QUICK SANDWICH

4 servings sliced cooked ham or chicken
4 slices toast
1 package (10 ounces) frozen asparagus spears, cooked and drained
1 can (10½ ounces) condensed cream of vegetable, celery, chicken, mushroom, or Cheddar cheese soup
¼ to ⅓ cup milk

Place chicken on toast; top with asparagus. In saucepan, combine soup and milk. Heat; stir now and then. Pour sauce over open-face sandwiches. 4 servings.

STEAK BARBECUE

1 pound thinly sliced sirloin, cut in strips
¼ cup chopped onion
1 large clove garlic, minced
1 teaspoon barbecue seasoning
2 tablespoons butter or margarine
1 can (10½ ounces) condensed tomato soup
⅓ cup water
4 frankfurter buns, split and toasted

Cook meat, onion, garlic, and barbecue seasoning in butter until meat is browned and onion is tender. Add soup and water. Cook for 10 minutes; stir often. Serve on buns. 4 servings.

BRUNCH PANCAKE SANDWICH

4 slices bacon
1 can (10½ ounces) condensed cream of chicken or mushroom soup
⅓ to ½ cup milk
4 hard-cooked eggs, sliced
2 tablespoons chopped pimiento
Pancakes

Cook bacon until crisp; remove and crumble; pour off drippings. Blend soup and milk; add bacon, eggs, and pimiento. Heat; stir now and then. Serve sandwiched between pancakes. 4 servings.

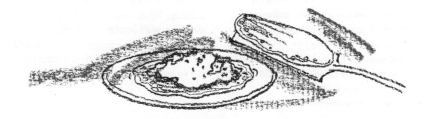

Dips and Spreads

When company is coming—or refrigerator-raiders descend—dips made with soup are creamy smooth, extra tasty and extra easy. A can of black bean soup or frozen condensed clam chowder or cream of shrimp soup—choose your favorites to form the basis for zesty dips and spreads that say welcome.

Serve soup dips with crackers and potato or corn chip dunkers. Or for a vitamin-packed change, use crisp carrot and celery sticks or cauliflowerets.

Many dip recipes double as spreads for the huge variety of breads and crackers on your supermarket shelf.

NOTE: When using frozen soup, allow for thawing time (30 minutes in hot water) before mixing.

SPANISH DIP

1 can (10 ounces) frozen condensed cream of shrimp soup, thawed
8 ounces cream cheese, softened
1 tablespoon finely chopped green pepper
1 tablespoon finely chopped onion
1 teaspoon chopped stuffed olives
Dash "Tabasco" sauce
Dash Worcestershire

With rotary beater or electric mixer, gradually blend soup into cream cheese. Beat *just* until smooth; *overbeating will make dip runny.* Blend in remaining ingredients. Chill. Makes about 2 cups. For extra tang, serve with corn chips.

SHRIMP DIP

1 can (10 ounces) frozen condensed
   cream of shrimp soup, thawed
8 ounces cream cheese, softened
1 teaspoon lemon juice
Dash garlic powder
Dash paprika

With an electric mixer or rotary beater, gradually blend soup and other ingredients; beat *just* until smooth. *Overbeating will make dip too thin.* Chill. Serve as a dip with crackers, chips, etc. Makes about 2 cups.

SHRIMP DILLY DIP

1 can (10 ounces) frozen condensed
   cream of shrimp soup, thawed
8 ounces cream cheese, softened
¼ cup chopped cucumber
2 tablespoons chopped onion
¼ teaspoon crushed dried dill
   leaves
4 to 5 drops "Tabasco" sauce

Gradually blend soup and other ingredients with electric mixer or rotary beater. Beat *just* until smooth; *overbeating will make dip too runny.* Chill. Makes about 2 cups.

NEW ENGLANDER'S SPECIAL

1 can (10¼ ounces) frozen condensed clam chowder (New England style), thawed
8 ounces cream cheese, softened
2 tablespoons minced onion
2 tablespoons ketchup

Gradually blend soup and other ingredients with rotary beater or electric mixer. Chill. Makes about 2 cups. Serve with oyster crackers for special seaside flavor.

SHRIMP BLUE CHEESE DIP

1 can (10 ounces) frozen condensed
   cream of shrimp soup, thawed
8 ounces cream cheese, softened
2 tablespoons crumbled blue cheese
1 tablespoon finely chopped onion
1 teaspoon sherry (optional)
Dash "Tabasco" sauce

Gradually blend soup and other ingredients with rotary beater or electric mixer. *Do not overbeat or dip will be too thin.* Chill. Makes about 2 cups.

CREAMY BEAN DUNK

8 ounces cream cheese, softened
1 can (10½ ounces) condensed
   black bean soup
2 tablespoons grated onion
Dash "Tabasco" sauce
Dash garlic powder

Beat cream cheese with rotary beater or electric mixer until smooth. Gradually add remaining ingredients; blend thoroughly. Chill. Makes about 2¼ cups.

CLAM DIGGERS' DUNK

1 can (10¼ ounces) frozen condensed clam chowder (New England style), thawed
8 ounces cream cheese, softened
1 can (4 ounces) mushrooms, drained and chopped
1 tablespoon minced onion
1 teaspoon Worcestershire
Dash cayenne pepper

Combine soup with other ingredients; beat until smooth with an electric mixer. Chill. Serve as a dip for crackers, potato chips, etc. Makes about 2 cups.

BACON 'N BEAN DIP

1 can (11¼ ounces) condensed bean with bacon soup
¼ cup chili sauce
2 tablespoons minced green pepper, if desired
1 teaspoon minced onion
1 teaspoon Worcestershire

Mix all ingredients; chill. Especially tasty with bacon wafers. If smoother dip is desired, beat in electric mixer or blender. May also be used as a sandwich spread, served on toast. Makes about 1½ cups.

CREAMY CHOWDER DIP

1 can (10¼ ounces) frozen condensed clam chowder (New England style), thawed
8 ounces cream cheese, softened
1 medium clove garlic, minced
½ teaspoon Worcestershire

Gradually blend soup with cream cheese, garlic, and Worcestershire with rotary beater or electric mixer. Beat until smooth. Chill. Makes about 2 cups.

DEVILED DELIGHT

8 ounces cream cheese, softened
1 can (10½ ounces) condensed tomato soup
2 cans (4½ ounces each) deviled ham
¼ cup finely chopped cucumber
2 teaspoons finely chopped green onion
1 small clove garlic, minced

Beat cream cheese until smooth with electric mixer or rotary beater. Add remaining ingredients; blend throughly. Chill. Makes about 2¼ cups. Serve as dip or spread for crackers, Melba toast, buttered bread.

Soups and the Freezer

Soups contribute to households with freezers in two ways.

First, frozen condensed soups are important freezer staples, to be kept on hand for superlative soups, and for use in making sauces, dips, and many dishes. The frozen condensed soups are: Clam Chowder (New England style), Green Pea with Ham, Oyster Stew, Cream of Potato, Cream of Shrimp, Old-Fashioned Vegetable with Beef. Recipes using these appear in other sections.

FROZEN SOUPS IN COOKING

In certain recipes, such as those for dips, you will need to thaw soup to use. The general rule for thawing is to remove soup from freezer just about 30 minutes before you want to use it in recipe; place unopened can in pan of hot water—and it should be thawed after 30 minutes.

It is not necessary to thaw frozen soup for a number of recipes, as you will note throughout the book. In most cases, you simply heat the soup with liquid and other ingredients until soup is thawed and dish is ready for eating.

The second contribution of soups to households with freezers is in helping with the preparation of special cooked dishes. If you're the lucky owner of a freezer, you know it's as easy to prepare a double amount of foods that freeze well—part to be eaten at once and part to be frozen. Many casseroles lend themselves especially well to this— and by using a can of soup for sauce, you can halve your cooking time. This is true also for creamed chicken and similar dishes to be frozen.

Research has shown that meats particularly freeze better when prepared with a sauce; this protects the meat from contact with air— and, therefore, aids in preventing off-flavors. Soup sauces are especially good for freezing because they retain their smooth consistency at low temperatures.

Other pointers to insure good results in freezing prepared foods are these:

1. Freeze only as much of a prepared food as you can use in one month or soon after. Generally, a fairly fast turnover is recommended by freezer specialists—rather than long storage of any food items.

2. Cool a cooked food as fast as possible and wrap it carefully so it is moistureproof.

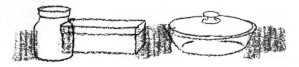

3. For packaging, you may place mixture in plastic freezer container or glass jar; leave 1-inch of head space at top because food will expand when frozen. Another method is to freeze and store the casserole mixture or similar food right in the casserole if you have one to spare. Or line a clean casserole with heavy duty aluminum foil, enough to wrap completely around the food and seal over the top. Pour in the food and seal foil with a double fold (press down tight against food). Place casserole in freezer until food is frozen solid. Then simply remove the foil-wrapped frozen food from the casserole . . . it will keep its shape and be protected in the freezer. When ready to serve the dish, remove it from foil (still frozen); put in pan to heat.

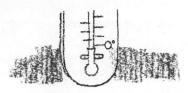

4. Freezing at 0°F. or lower is important to success with any kind of food. Put unfrozen foods in the fastest freezing area or in direct contact with freezer walls or shelves and away from already frozen foods. Place packages so air can circulate among them. Do not overload freezer with a large number of foods to be frozen at once.

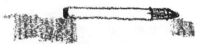

5. Label each package with date. name of product, and number of servings.

6. Freeze in one package an average amount for serving your family. Large amounts take a long time to freeze—and to heat later on for serving (unless thawed completely before re-heating). Food in a large casserole may burn around the edges before it is warm in the center.

7. When preparing casseroles or stews for freezing, shorten cooking time slightly to allow for the additional cooking which takes place during re-heating.

8. To prepare a frozen main dish for serving, you may thaw it in the refrigerator—and bake as usual as soon as thawed. Or you may heat the frozen item in the oven—allowing longer heating time than specified in the original recipe (you will need to check dish during baking since no specific rule for increased baking time can be given for all dishes).

A number of dishes throughout this book have been tested for successful freezing. These include (see index):

Macaroni and Cheese—Family Style
Old Fashioned Meat Loaf (leave off topping)
Tomato Beef Stew (do not flour meat; leave out potatoes and thyme)
Seafood Newburg

The following recipes also freeze well:

STROGANOFF

1 pound round steak, cut into thin strips
½ cup chopped onion
2 tablespoons butter or margarine
1 can (10½ ounces) condensed cream of mushroom soup
¼ cup water
½ cup sour cream
½ teaspoon paprika
2 cups cooked noodles

Brown steak and onion in butter. Stir in soup, water, sour cream, and paprika. Cover; cook over low heat 45 minutes or until meat is tender. Stir often. Serve over noodles. 4 servings.

CHILI MEATBALLS

1 pound ground beef
2 tablespoons fine dry bread crumbs
2 tablespoons finely chopped onion
1 egg, slightly beaten
1 teaspoon chili powder
¼ teaspoon salt
1 can (10¾ ounces) condensed tomato soup
⅓ cup water
1 small clove garlic, minced

Mix beef, bread crumbs, onion, egg, ½ teaspoon chili powder, and salt; shape into 16 meatballs. In skillet, brown meatballs; pour off fat. Stir in soup, water, garlic, and remaining chili powder. Cover; cook over low heat 20 minutes. Stir now and then. 4 servings.

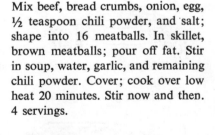

All About Soups

Soup enhances mealtime pleasure today as it has from the beginning of time.

With the modern condensed soups, you have this favorite food on hand around the clock—whether winter or summer. Try a cup or bowlful for that something new to brighten breakfast or a snacktime. Send it in a lunch box to add a note of warmth. Dress it up for a party—using a special soup mate or a gala garnish.

The following chapters cover almost every phase of modern-day soup service. Many recipes and menus are given for family meals and guest occasions.

Nourishing Soup Through the Day

Soup can work a full day in helping you plan sound menus. Look over the following mealtime suggestions for tips on breakfast through supper:

1. CEREAL SURPRISE: Suppose, for example, Bob or Jane hits a breakfast snag. Cereal suddenly remains untouched, and the morning meal seems a bore. A bowl of Scotch broth with its nubbins of barley, bright vegetables, and meat pieces may be just the interesting contrast in taste and texture that is needed.

WARM-UP BREAKFAST	SUNNY STARTER
Sliced Orange	Grapefruit Sections
Bowl of Scotch Broth	French Toast
Toast and Jelly	Mug of Tomato Soup (made
Crisp Bacon Curls	with milk)
Milk	

2. MILK BONUS: Teen-aged Sally suddenly leaves milk behind; or her father, a man of meat-and-potatoes tastes, ignores the fact that adults need a pint of milk a day, too. Most condensed soups can be heated with milk instead of water; skim milk or instant non-fat dry milk fill dieters' needs.

MILK BONUS SNACKS	ANY DAY DINNER
Cream of Mushroom Mug	Cream of Shrimp Soup
Cheese and Cracker Squares	Ham Steak Green Beans
• • •	Salad with Easy Russian Dressing
Cream of Tomato Cup	Apple Strudel (frozen)
Cinnamon Toast	Sliced Cheese

3. VEGETABLE WELCOME: Billy balks at vegetables. For him, lunch or supper might start with a bowl of any one of the vegetable soups.

LUNCH BOX WINNER
Minestrone (in vacuum bottle)
Tuna Fish Sandwich
Brownies   Fruit
Milk

SUPPER SPECIAL
Vegetable Soup
Barbecued Frankfurters
Apple Salad
Cookies   Milk

4. MEATLESS MENUS: Aside from the basic food values, soups help meet other special nutritional needs. On fast days or budget days, meatless meals may be planned around soups. Count on these meatless kinds: black bean, Cheddar cheese, cream soups (vegetable, asparagus, celery, mushroom), green pea, tomato, tomato rice, vegetarian vegetable, clam chowder (both styles); cream of potato, cream of shrimp, oyster stew.

FRIDAY DINNER
Purée Mongole*
Saucy Fish Fillets*
Baked Potatoes   Buttered Broccoli
Berries in Tart Shells   Cream

GOURMET BUFFET
Clam Chowder
Tuna Noodle Casserole*
Baked Stuffed Tomatoes
Spice Cake

5. PICKUPS: Secretary Sue wants a work-break at midmorning or midafternoon. So does Mrs. Homemaker—and almost everyone else. For many, this should be a low-calorie pause, which provides a quick pickup. Soup taken as a "work-break" has lasting advantages. Beef broth and consomme are particularly convenient and low-calorie choices, served hot or cold.

6. SOOTHING SOUP: Soup makes a "warming welcome home" to youngsters after school (try vegetable or green pea for hearty eating) . . . a great midnight snack after a movie (cosmopolitans take French onion) . . . good companion for travelers (chicken noodle and vegetable beef, the favorites) . . . and the nightcap that brings tranquil dreams (cream of chicken or chicken with rice).

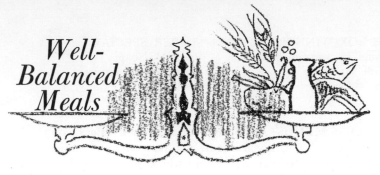

Well-Balanced Meals

As a modern homemaker, one of your first aims in keeping your family healthy is to provide well-balanced, nourishing meals.

The supermarkets where you shop are treasure houses—stocked with tempting foods of every kind. When selecting from these, you will find the many kinds of condensed soups are helpful again and again.

From clear broths to hearty chowders, they contain a range of nutrients as is to be expected.

Most soups contain well-balanced calories . . . they afford a good share of the required nutrients for the calories contributed.

With all the different kinds of condensed soups—and all the ingredients that go into them—there's good variety for balanced meals. Look over the many soups and see how they fit into the basic four food groups:

1. MILK SOUPS:	2. MEAT & LEGUME SOUPS:	3. VEGETABLE SOUPS:	4. CEREAL SOUPS:
Cheddar Cheese	Bean with Bacon	Chicken	Beef Noodle
Clam Chowder	Beef	Vegetable	Chicken & Stars
(Frozen New	Chili Beef	Clam Chowder	Chicken Gumbo
England Style)	Consomme	(Manhattan	Chicken Noodle
Cream of	Green Pea	Style)	Chicken with
Asparagus	Green Pea with	Cream of	Rice
Cream of Celery	Ham (Frozen)	Asparagus	Noodles &
Cream of	Pepper Pot	Cream of Potato	Ground Beef
Chicken	Scotch Broth	Green Pea	Scotch Broth
Cream of	Split Pea with	Minestrone	Tomato Rice
Mushroom	Ham	Old Fashioned	Turkey Noodle
Cream of Potato	Vegetable Beef	Vegetable	
Cream of Shrimp		Scotch Broth	
(Frozen)		Tomato	
Cream of		Tomato Rice	
Vegetable		Turkey Vegetable	
Oyster Stew		Vegetable	
(Frozen)		Vegetable Bean	
		Vegetable Beef	
		Vegetarian	
		Vegetable	

Better Breakfasts

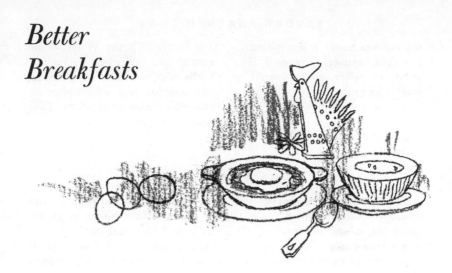

Those who know the joys of soup for breakfast—hearty, warming, invigorating—crow about their eye-openers.

Soup gives bonus flavor to more usual breakfast foods. Try eggs poached in soup. Here's breakfast news that nurtures the spirit, too!

There is also soup in a bowl or mug, heated as usual, perhaps with a generous pat of butter melting on top. Serve with crisp toast or muffin; add browned bacon or golden sausage, and fruit to round out a happy start for the day.

COLD DAY BREAKFAST
Grapefruit Half
Chicken Vegetable Soup
French Toast
Cocoa

SPRING DAY BREAKFAST
Fruit in Season
Savory Poached Eggs*
  on English Muffins
Milk or Coffee

SUMMER BREAKFAST
Half Cantaloupe
Tomato Soup (made with milk)
  with Corn Flakes on top
Buttered Toast   Bacon
Milk or Coffee

AUTUMN BREAKFAST
Sliced Orange
Vegetable Beef Soup
Coffee Cake
Milk or Coffee

SAVORY POACHED EGGS

2 tablespoons butter or margarine
1 can (10½ ounces) condensed cream of celery, chicken, or mushroom soup
½ cup milk
6 eggs
3 English muffins (split, toasted, and buttered)

Melt butter in heavy skillet. Blend in soup and milk; heat to boiling. Gently slip eggs into soup sauce; cook over low heat until whites are firm. Place eggs on muffins. Pour sauce over eggs. 6 servings.

CAMPBELLED EGGS

1 can (10½ ounces) condensed Cheddar cheese, cream of vegetable, celery, chicken, or mushroom soup
8 eggs, slightly beaten
Dash pepper
2 tablespoons butter or margarine, melted

Blend soup, eggs, and pepper; pour egg mixture into butter in skillet. Cook over low heat until eggs are set; stir gently. 4 to 6 servings. If desired, substitute a can of thawed frozen condensed cream of shrimp soup for any of the above.

CREAMED BRUNCH BEEF

1 package (4 ounces) sliced dried beef
¼ cup chopped onion
2 tablespoons butter or margarine
1 can (10½ ounces) condensed cream of celery soup
½ cup milk
4 slices toast

Rinse dried beef in hot water; drain. Brown beef and onion in butter. Stir in soup and milk. Heat; stir often. Serve on hot toast. 4 servings.

DON FAR TONG (Egg Drop Soup)

2 cans (10½ ounces each) condensed beef broth
2 soup cans water
½ medium bay leaf
1 egg

Combine soup, water, and bay leaf. Bring to a boil. Beat egg slightly; slowly pour it in a thin stream into soup, stirring constantly. Remove bay leaf. Egg should form thin threads. Serve with toast 4 to 6 servings.

Tomato Rice Soup, Hoagie, Fruit
Oyster Stew, Jellied Vegetable Salad, Finger Sandwiches

Magic Menu Maker
for Lunches
and
Lunch Box Meals

Soup and sandwiches are an American lunchtime favorite—as right nutritionally as they are good to eat. Soups offer a good way to add vegetables, meat, and/or milk to noon meals.

Does someone in your home carry a lunch? If so, your household is like 40% of all others . . . where someone carries a lunch at least every other weekday. Here are some tips on packing lunches which may be helpful to you:

1. About one third of the day's food needs should be included—so plan a well-balanced meal with a few extras to satisfy your "luncher". Select favorite foods and food combinations—one of the best is soup and sandwiches. Plan a "surprise" to include as often as possible —such as salted nuts or mints. Plenty of paper napkins and colorful straws for sipping milk are other "inviting" touches for the lunch box.

2. For sandwiches, use a variety of fillings and breads. If you make up sandwiches the night before they're to be eaten, keep them refrigerated until you pack the lunch. Wrap sandwiches in moistureproof, clear lunch box wrap material or foil as soon as they are made.

3. Wrap lettuce or other moist fillings, such as sliced tomatoes, separately. Do not include salad-type meat fillings for sandwiches unless the lunch can be stored in a cool place—and will only be held for a short time.

4. Always have one hot dish. You're sure of pleasing if you include a vacuum bottle of hot soup. Any of the condensed soups are good to carry. And many kinds may be prepared with milk—a nutritional plus. A wide-mouth vacuum bottle is ideal for soup—easy to pour into and to eat from. Make sure the soup's hot before packing (rinse the vacuum bottle with hot water before pouring in soup). Be sure to send along a soup spoon or a long-handled spoon for eating right from the bottle.

Cioppino   Page 162

MATCH OR MIX—
ONE ITEM FROM EACH COLUMN—

SOUPS	SANDWICHES	DESSERTS	TIPS FOR LUNCH BOX
Cream of Asparagus	Meat loaf on hard roll	Fig bars	Cut sandwich roll in half for easy eating
Bean with Bacon	Sliced ham and lettuce on rye bread	Apple and pretzels	Wrap lettuce for sandwich in waxed paper
Beef	Swiss cheese on whole wheat bread	Peaches (fresh or canned)	Pack cole slaw in container with lid
Beef Noodle	Cheese and crackers (combine when eating)	Cherry pie	Use the individual-size frozen pies
Black Bean	Tomato and bacon on whole wheat bread	Pineapple (fresh or canned)	Spread bread with butter; prevents moist filling from soaking into bread
Beef Broth or Consomme	Sharp cheese and lettuce on white bread	Fruit tapioca (in covered container)	Add a small bag of salted nuts
Cream of Celery	Tuna or salmon salad on hard roll	Grapefruit sections	Cut unpeeled fruit into wedges
Cream of Chicken	Ham and cheese— "double decker"	Grapes and oatmeal cookies	Make it white and dark bread sandwich
Cream of Potato	Sliced turkey or roast pork	Fruit cocktail	Put in cranberry sauce for sandwich
Chicken Gumbo	Date-nut bread and butter	Orange and macaroons	Peel and section orange; pack in sandwich bag
Chicken Noodle	Sliced egg and bacon on whole wheat bread	Molasses cookies	Add radishes or green pepper for crunch
Chicken with Rice	Cottage cheese and chopped olives on cracked wheat bread	Chocolate chip cookies	Use clear lunch box wrap for sandwiches
Chicken Vegetable	Peanut butter and jelly on white bread	Stewed prunes (in container)	Include a few crackers to go with soup
Chili Beef	Sliced cheese and pickle relish	Banana	Put in lettuce for sandwich and carrot sticks for nibbling
Clam Chowder	Egg salad on white bread	Cherries (fresh or canned)	Pickles and olives go well with sandwich

FOR GOOD LUNCHES AT HOME OR AWAY

SOUPS	SANDWICHES	DESSERTS	TIPS FOR LUNCH BOX
Green Pea	Ham salad on poppyseed roll	Apricots (fresh or canned)	Include plastic fork and spoon
Minestrone	Bologna sandwich on hard roll	Orange sections (in paper cup)	Freeze sandwiches for lunch boxes
Cream of Mushroom	Corned beef on rye bread	Applesauce and a doughnut	Tuck in, for a snack, small box raisins
Pepper Pot	Cream cheese and dried beef on white bread	Pears (fresh or canned)	Use glass jars with tops for desserts
Scotch Broth	Cream cheese and olive on rye bread	Canned mixed fruit	Include a bag of popcorn
Split Pea with Ham	Chicken spread and stuffed olives on roll	Coconut cup cake	Put in lettuce for sandwich
Tomato	Hot dog (tie it with string and put it in vacuum of hot soup; take out of soup to eat on a bun)	Applesauce cake	Celery and carrot sticks are crunchy
Tomato Rice	Cold roast beef on white bread	Baked apple (in container)	Be sure to include a napkin or two
Turkey Noodle	Deviled ham and tomato on whole wheat bread	Date and nut bars	Wrap slices of tomato for sandwich in foil
Turkey Vegetable	Sliced ham and cheese	Candy bar	Add cole slaw
Cream of Vegetable	Chive cheese on pumpernickel bread	Gingerbread squares	Keep vacuum bottle clean and "sweet"; rinse with baking soda solution
Vegetable	Bacon, lettuce, sliced tomato on soft roll	Brownies	Wrap sandwich items separately; let "luncher" put together
Vegetable Bean	Lunch meat on rye	Gingersnaps	Put in pickles
Vegetable Beef	Cheese cracker and peanut butter "sandwiches"	Plums (fresh or canned)	Include a hard-cooked egg
Vegetarian Vegetable	Sliced chicken on whole wheat bread	Chocolate cup cake	Put mayonnaise or mustard in small piece of foil

Supper Soups

The simplest, most exciting supper in the world may be yours in a large soup bowl. Such a supper can be as easy as this: For each serving prepare a hamburger, a few meatballs, or sliced franks. Heat a generous portion of your favorite hearty soup. Place a portion of meat in the soup bowl; ladle the soup over. Or prepare any of the following substantial soup-supper recipes as tasty main dishes.

SUPPER SOUP MENUS

Rosy Chili and Beef Soup*
Green Salad   Corn Muffins
Raspberry Turnovers (frozen)

Chicken Pea Soup Bowl*
Brown 'n' Serve Rolls
Fruit Salad   Cookies

Seafood and Tomato Bowl*
Crackers and Cheese   Relishes
Cherry Strudel (frozen)

Tomato Minestrone Meal*
Egg and Green Pepper Salad
Toasted Italian Bread
Spumoni

ROSY CHILI AND BEEF SOUP

½ pound ground beef
2 tablespoons chopped onion
1 teaspoon chili powder
½ teaspoon salt
1 tablespoon butter or margarine
1 can (10½ ounces) condensed tomato soup
1 can (10¾ ounces) condensed beef soup
1½ soup cans water

Combine beef, onion, chili powder, and salt; shape into 12 small meatballs. In saucepan, brown meatballs in butter. Add soups and water. Heat; stir often. 4 servings.

138

OLD-FASHIONED VEGETABLE-BACON SOUP

3 slices bacon, cut in half
¼ cup slivered green pepper
1 can (10¼ ounces) frozen condensed old-fashioned vegetable with beef soup
1 soup can water
⅛ teaspoon tarragon, crushed

Cook bacon until crisp; remove and crumble. Pour off all but about 1 tablespoon drippings; add green pepper and cook until tender. Add soup, water, and tarragon. Heat until soup is thawed; stir often. Garnish with bacon. 2 to 3 servings.

SWISS POTATO SOUP

1 can (10¼ ounces) frozen condensed cream of potato soup
1 soup can milk
⅛ teaspoon dry mustard
½ cup shredded Swiss cheese
1 tablespoon chopped parsley

Combine soup, milk, and mustard. Heat until soup thaws. Add cheese and parsley. Heat until cheese melts; stir often. 3 servings.
NOTE: For thinner soup, use ½ soup can milk and ½ soup can water.

HEARTY FRANKFURTER SOUP

2 frankfurters, thinly sliced
2 tablespoons chopped onion
1 tablespoon butter or margarine
1 can (10¾ ounces) condensed tomato rice soup
1 soup can water

Brown frankfurters and onion in butter. Add soup and water. Heat; stir often. 2 to 3 servings.

CREAMY VEGETABLE SALMON SOUP

½ cup thinly sliced cucumber
2 tablespoons chopped onion
⅛ teaspoon minced dill leaves
1 tablespoon butter or margarine
1 can (10¾ ounces) condensed cream of vegetable soup
1 cup water
⅓ cup sour cream
1 can (8 ounces) salmon, drained and flaked

Cook cucumber, onion, and dill in butter until partially tender. Blend in remaining ingredients. Heat, *but do not boil.* Stir often. 3 to 4 servings.

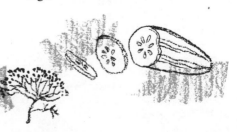

CHICKEN 'N' LIMA SOUP

1 can (10¾ ounces) condensed
  chicken vegetable soup
1 soup can milk
1 cup cooked lima beans
4 slices bacon, cooked and
  crumbled

Combine soup, milk, and lima beans. Heat; stir. Just before serving, add crumbled bacon. 4 servings. If desired, garnish with sliced hard-cooked egg.

TUNA POTATO CHOWDER

2 slices bacon
¼ cup chopped onion
2 tablespoons finely chopped
  green pepper
1 can (10¼ ounces) frozen condensed cream of potato soup
½ soup can milk
½ soup can water
Dash ground mace
1 can (7 ounces) tuna, drained
  and flaked

Fry bacon. Place on paper towel to drain; crumble. Pour off all but 2 tablespoons drippings. Add onion and green pepper; cook until tender. Add remaining ingredients. Heat until soup is thawed; *do not boil;* stir often. Garnish with crumbled bacon and paprika, if desired. 4 servings.

CHICKEN BEEF BOWL

1 package (4 ounces) sliced dried
  beef
½ cup chopped onion
2 tablespoons butter or margarine
1 can (10½ ounces) condensed
  cream of celery soup
1 can (10½ ounces) condensed
  cream of mushroom soup
1 soup can milk
1 soup can water
1 can (10½ ounces) condensed
  chicken noodle soup
1 package (10 ounces) frozen
  succotash, cooked and drained
Dash pepper

Shred dried beef; rinse in hot water; drain. In large saucepan, brown beef and onion in butter. Blend in cream soups, milk, and water; add remaining ingredients. Heat; stir often. 6 to 8 servings.

LOBSTER MUSHROOM SOUP

¼ cup chopped onion
2 tablespoons butter or margarine
2 cans (10½ ounces each) condensed cream of mushroom or celery soup
1 soup can milk
1 soup can water
1 cup flaked cooked lobster (or 6½-ounce can, drained)
2 tablespoons chopped parsley
Dash pepper
Dash paprika

Cook onion in butter until tender. Blend in soup and remaining ingredients. Heat; stir often. Garnish each serving with paprika. 6 to 8 servings. NOTE: Substitute crab, salmon, shrimp, or tuna for lobster.

SPLIT PEA 'N TOMATO

1 can (11¼ ounces) condensed split pea with ham soup
1 can (10½ ounces) condensed tomato soup
1 cup milk
1 cup water

Blend soups. Gradually stir in milk and water. Heat; stir often. 4 to 6 servings.

CHICKEN PEA SOUP BOWL

1 small onion, sliced
⅛ teaspoon nutmeg
2 tablespoons butter or margarine
1 can (10½ ounces) condensed cream of chicken soup
1 can (11¼ ounces) condensed green pea soup
1 can (5 ounces) boned chicken or turkey, or 1 cup diced cooked chicken or turkey
1 cup cooked sliced carrots
1 cup chopped spinach
1½ soup cans water

Cook onion and nutmeg in butter until onion is tender. Add remaining ingredients. Cover; simmer 5 minutes; stir often. 5 to 6 servings.

SOUP PLUS

A pattern recipe to use as you like with foods you have on hand.

½ cup cooked meat, cut in strips
1 tablespoon butter or margarine
1 can any Campbell's Soup
1 soup can milk or water
½ cup cooked vegetables

Cook meat in butter until lightly browned. Add remaining ingredients. Heat; stir often. 2 to 3 servings.

BEAN AND SAUSAGE SOUP

1 or 2 small sausage links (about 2 ounces)
1 can (11¼ ounces) condensed bean with bacon soup
1 soup can water
Cubes of red apple

Cut sausage into ½-inch slices; brown in saucepan; pour off drippings. Blend in soup and water. Heat; stir often. Top each serving with apple cubes. 2 to 3 servings.

MINESTRONE MEAL

3 sausage links
2 cans (10¾ ounces each) condensed minestrone soup
1 can (10½ ounces) condensed tomato soup
3 soup cans water
Croutons

Cut sausage into penny-slices. Brown in saucepan; drain. Add soups and water. Heat; stir often. Top with croutons. 6 to 8 servings.

SEAFOOD AND TOMATO BOWL

¼ cup chopped onion
1 small clove garlic, minced
1 tablespoon butter or margarine
1 can (10¾ ounces) condensed clam chowder (Manhattan style)
1 can (10¾ ounces) condensed tomato rice soup
1½ soup cans water
1 can (7 ounces) tuna, drained and flaked
2 tablespoons chopped parsley

Cook onion and garlic in butter until onion is tender. Add remaining ingredients. Heat; stir often. 4 to 6 servings.

SAUSAGE MINESTRONE

2 or 3 sausage links (about 3
  ounces), cut into thick slices
1 can (10¾ ounces) condensed
  minestrone soup
1 soup can water

Brown sausage slices lightly; pour off drippings. Add soup and water. Heat; stir often. 2 to 3 servings.

CHICKEN CORN CHOWDER

1 can (10½ ounces) condensed
  cream of chicken soup
2 soup cans milk
1 can (10½ ounces) condensed
  chicken noodle soup
1 can (1 pound) cream-style corn
1 can (5 ounces) boned chicken, or
  1 cup diced cooked chicken

Blend cream of chicken soup and milk. Add remaining ingredients. Heat; *do not boil.* 6 to 8 servings.

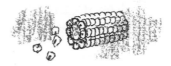

BACON AND VEGETABLE POTAGE

½ cup Canadian bacon, cut in strips
¼ cup chopped onion
⅛ teaspoon ground sage
1 tablespoon butter or margarine
1 can (10½ ounces) condensed
  cream of chicken soup
1 can (10¾ ounces) condensed
  cream of vegetable soup
1 soup can water
½ soup can milk
½ cup cooked chopped spinach

Cook bacon, onion, and sage in butter until bacon is browned and onion is tender. Blend in remaining ingredients. Heat; stir often. 4 to 6 servings.

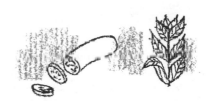

FRANK AND BEAN SOUP

2 to 4 frankfurters, thinly sliced
1 tablespoon butter or margarine
1 can (11¼ ounces) condensed
  bean with bacon soup
1 can (11¼ ounces) condensed
  green pea soup
1 soup can milk
1 soup can water

Lightly brown frankfurter slices in butter. Blend in remaining ingredients. Heat; *do not boil.* 4 to 6 servings. If desired, 1 cup diced cooked carrots may also be added.

Youngsters
Like Soup

From the toddling stage on, kids love soup. Among one-year-olds, 4 out of 10 eat soup; 7 out of 10 two-year-olds eat soup!

From split style to swirly, there's a soup for all kidfolk. Soup fits into menus for youngsters year 'round . . . for lunchboxes, snacks, camp-outs, and cook-outs.

"GROWING-UP" SOUPS may be given to your baby when he's ready for soft chewing foods. Some recommended by doctors include: cream of asparagus, cream of celery, beef, beef noodle, chicken noodle, chicken with rice, green pea, Scotch broth, tomato, vegetable, vegetable beef, vegetarian vegetable, chicken vegetable, and turkey noodle.

SPLIT STYLE is an easy way for the very young one to eat soup. Make up soup with milk and heat thoroughly. Pour the nutritious broth into a cup for drinking; spoon the colorful solids onto a plate for eating.

BIRTHDAY SOUP: Gay bowls of cream soup take on a party air when topped with a glowing birthday candle (set on a floating round of toast or a cracker). First top the cracker with a small ball of cream cheese or peanut butter. Poke the end of the candle into it and carefully slip the cracker onto the top of the soup. Then light up the candle.

SWIRLY SOUPS: Exciting to do and nourishing too. Let the youngsters swirl or write on the soup surface this way. Prepare soup as usual and pour into bowls. Slowly pour light cream, milk, reconstituted dry milk, or evaporated milk from a pitcher, back and forth across the soup. Stir with a soup spoon to make initials, animals, faces, or pretty marbled effects.

SNIPPETS: Good eating with soup are snippets of cheese. These are simply animals, numbers, stars, or other shapes that youngsters cut with cookie cutters from slices of process cheese. These float atop soup.

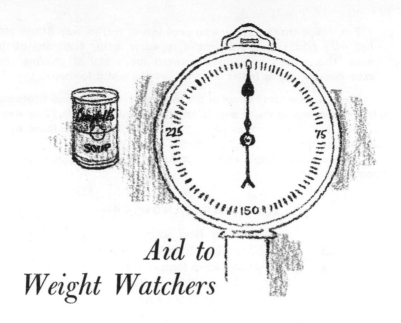

Aid to
Weight Watchers

Calorie-conscious folks (wanting to lose or gain weight) can look over the following groupings of soup to see what the calories are. CALORIES PER AVERAGE SERVING OF CONDENSED SOUP, 3 SERVINGS PER CAN (SOUP PREPARED WITH WATER):

25 to 50 calories: Beef broth, chicken gumbo, chicken with rice, and consomme.

50 to 75 calories: Cream of asparagus, beef noodle, cream of celery, cream of chicken, chicken noodle, chicken vegetable, clam chowder (Manhattan style), onion, Scotch broth, tomato, turkey noodle, turkey vegetable, vegetable, vegetable beef, vegetarian vegetable, frozen old-fashioned vegetable with beef.

75 to 100 calories: Beef, black bean, minestrone, pepper pot, cream of vegetable, frozen cream of potato, tomato rice, vegetable bean.

100 to 125 calories: Green pea, cream of mushroom, frozen clam chowder (New England style), frozen green pea with ham, frozen oyster stew.

125 to 150 calories: Bean with bacon, Cheddar cheese, chili beef, frozen cream of shrimp, split pea.

For THE SLENDER: Those who need lots of fuel to keep fit will also find soup a help. It is a delightful appetizer at the beginning of the meal. Too, it may be enjoyed between meals and at bedtime (for extra calories, a little butter or cream may be added to soup).

Low-CALORIE TIPS: Many of the soups team up with sandwiches and salads or desserts to make well-balanced, low-calorie meals. Two soups . . . beef broth and consomme . . . are low enough in calories to be listed among the "free foods" for dieters to enjoy anytime.

Here are two simple menus for low-calorie meals, each equal to about 400 calories.

SOUP AND SANDWICH

¾ cup Beef Soup
Open-Face Sliced Egg Sandwich on
Rye Bread, Green Pepper Garnish
1 Glass Skim Milk or Buttermilk
1 Portion Fresh Fruit

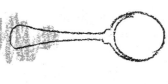

SOUP AND SALAD

¾ cup Cream of Celery Soup,
Prepared with Milk, 2 Saltines
Cold plate—2 ounces Sliced Lean Meat,
Chicken, or Turkey
Sliced Tomato and Dill Pickle Garnish
½ cup Orange and Grapefruit Compote

Low-calorie soups can be extra-flavorful, as in these recipes:

BEEF BROTH CHABLIS

1 can (10½ ounces) condensed beef broth
1 soup can water
2 tablespoons Chablis or other dry white wine (optional)

Combine all ingredients. Place in refrigerator for at least 4 hours. Serve in chilled cups or glasses. 3 servings. Calories per serving: about 35.

ENERGY BOOSTER

1 can (10½ ounces) condensed
   tomato soup
1 soup can water
1 bay leaf
¼ teaspoon celery salt

Combine all ingredients. Heat; simmer a few minutes to blend flavors. Remove bay leaf. 3 mugs. Calories per serving: about 75.

CRESS BROTH

1 can (10½ ounces) condensed
   beef broth
½ to 1 soup can water
2 tablespoons minced watercress
Lemon wedges

Combine beef broth, water, and watercress. Place in refrigerator for at least 4 hours. Serve in chilled mugs or bowls; garnish with lemon wedges. 3 servings. Calories per serving: about 35.
VARIATION: Try this with tomato soup, too.

SPINACH TOMATO SOUP

1 cup chopped fresh spinach
1 tablespoon butter or margarine
1 can (10½ ounces) condensed
   tomato soup
1 soup can milk or water
¼ teaspoon ground nutmeg

Cook spinach in butter 5 minutes. Blend in soup, liquid, and nutmeg. Heat; stir now and then. 3 servings. Calories per serving: about 112.

CHICKEN VEGETABLE V-8

1 can (10¾ ounces) condensed
   chicken vegetable soup
½ soup can V-8
½ soup can water

Combine soup, V-8, and water. Heat; stir now and then. 3 servings. Calories per serving: about 74.

BROTH PICK-UP

1 can (10½ ounces) condensed
   beef broth
1 can (10½ ounces) condensed
   tomato soup
1 soup can water
½ teaspoon lemon juice
⅛ teaspoon sweet basil

Combine all ingredients. Heat; simmer a few minutes. Stir now and then. 3 to 4 servings. Calories per serving for 3: about 93; for 4: about 69.

Appetizer Soups

"Soup puts the heart at ease, calms down the violence of hunger, eliminates the tensions of the day, and awakens and refines the appetite."—Escoffier

Soup, hot or chilled, sets the mood for the meal to come. Soup can breathe of spring, or bring warmth to a cold winter's evening. Cool jellied consomme revives summer appetites, and robust soups add substance to an autumn meal. Bright soup can give the color contrast needed for a pale table setting. Clear broth is the gourmet's choice to set off elegant dinners. A tureen of soup makes a popular addition to a buffet, and the most welcome centerpiece of all, when the family gathers at the table. Happy is the family that can answer yes to

> "Do daily soups
> Your dinners introduce?"—John Gay

TOMATO MINESTRONE

1 can (10¾ ounces) condensed
    minestrone soup
½ soup can water
½ soup can tomato juice

Combine all ingredients. Heat. 2 to 3 servings.

NUTMEG MUG

1 can (11¼ ounces) condensed
  green pea soup
1 soup can water or milk
⅛ to ¼ teaspoon ground nutmeg
Orange slices, cut in quarters

Combine soup, water or milk, and nutmeg. Heat; stir now and then. Serve in mugs or cups; garnish with orange slices. 2 to 3 servings.

WHITE PUFF PEA SOUP

1 can (10½ ounces) frozen condensed green pea with ham soup
1 soup can water
Dash ground cloves
⅓ cup heavy cream
1 teaspoon grated orange rind

Combine soup, water, and cloves in saucepan. Heat until soup is thawed; stir now and then. Whip cream; fold in orange rind. Top each serving with a dab of orange whipped cream. 2 to 3 servings.

SOUP ITALIANO

1 can (11¼ ounces) condensed
  green pea soup
1 can (10½ ounces) condensed
  tomato soup
1½ soup cans water
2 tablespoons Chianti or other dry
  red wine (optional)
⅛ teaspoon Italian herb blend

Blend soups; add remaining ingredients. Cook over low heat 10 minutes; stir often. 4 servings. Serve with crackers spread with Mozzarella cheese, sprinkled with oregano and browned under the broiler.

CREOLE SOUP

2 slices bacon
2 tablespoons chopped onion
1 can (10¾ ounces) condensed
  tomato rice soup
1 soup can water
½ cup cooked cut green beans

Cook bacon until crisp; remove and crumble. Pour off excess drippings. Add onion; cook until tender. Add soup, water, green beans, and most of bacon. Heat; stir. Sprinkle with bacon. 2 to 3 servings.

CHILLED MINTED PEA SOUP

1 can (11¼ ounces) condensed
  green pea soup
1 soup can milk
¼ cup light cream
½ teaspoon dried mint flakes,
  crushed

Blend all ingredients. Chill at least 4 hours. 3 to 4 servings.

ROSY TURKEY NOODLE SOUP

1 can (10½ ounces) condensed
  turkey noodle soup
½ soup can water
½ soup can V-8

Combine all ingredients. Heat. 2 to 3 servings.

CHEESE–TOMATO

1 can (11 ounces) condensed
  Cheddar cheese soup
1 can (10½ ounces) condensed
  tomato soup
2 soup cans water

Stir cheese soup until smooth; gradually blend in tomato soup and water. Heat; stir often. 4 to 6 servings.

SUPPER PARTY STARTER

1 can (10½ ounces) condensed
  beef broth
1 soup can water
2 tablespoons wine (sauterne,
  sherry, rose, or Burgundy)
Orange or lemon slices, clove
  studded

Combine beef broth and water; add wine. Heat a few minutes to blend flavors. Float clove-studded orange or lemon slices in broth for a colorful touch of that special something guests appreciate. 2 to 3 servings.

CONSOMME JULIENNE

1 cup vegetables cut in thin strips
  (carrot, onion, green pepper, leek,
  parsnip)
1 tablespoon butter or margarine
2 cans (10½ ounces each) condensed consomme
2 soup cans water

Choose vegetables for variety in color and flavor. Cook in butter with cover on, over very low heat, until tender but still firm. Add consomme and water. Heat; do not boil. 6 to 8 servings.

SAVORY CHILLED MUSHROOM BOWL

1 can (10½ ounces) condensed
   cream of mushroom soup
1 soup can milk
1 teaspoon minced chives or
   chopped fresh dill
Sour cream, if desired

Blend soup, milk, and seasoning. Chill at least 4 hours. Serve in chilled bowls. Garnish with dollop of sour cream. 2 to 3 servings.

POTATO BROCCOLI BOWL

1 can (10¼ ounces) frozen
   condensed cream of potato soup
1 soup can milk
Dash ground nutmeg
Dash pepper
½ cup chopped cooked broccoli

In saucepan, combine soup, milk, and seasonings. Heat; stir now and then. Do not boil. Add broccoli; heat. 3 to 4 servings.

CREAMY POTATO POTAGE

½ cup finely chopped cucumber
2 tablespoons chopped green onion
2 tablespoons butter or margarine
1 can (10¼ ounces) frozen condensed cream of potato soup
1 soup can water
⅛ teaspoon paprika
⅓ cup sour cream

Cook cucumber and green onion in butter until tender. Add soup, water, and paprika. Heat; stir now and then. Blend in sour cream. 2 to 3 servings. To serve as cold soup, prepare as above, then chill about 4 hours. Stir in ½ to 1 cup milk before serving.

QUICK RHODE ISLAND CHOWDER

2 tablespoons chopped onion
⅛ teaspoon leaf thyme, crushed
2 tablespoons butter or margarine
1 can (10¼ ounces) frozen
   condensed clam chowder
   (New England style)
1 soup can milk
½ cup cooked peas

In saucepan, cook onion and thyme in butter until onion is tender. Add soup and milk. Heat; stir now and then. Do not boil. Add peas; heat. 2 to 3 servings.

CHILLED PARSLEY-SHRIMP SOUP

1 can (10 ounces) frozen condensed
   cream of shrimp soup
1 soup can water
1 tablespoon chopped parsley
½ small clove garlic, minced

Combine all ingredients. Heat until soup is thawed; stir often. Chill at least 4 hours and serve as a cooling appetizer. 2 to 3 servings.

151

SPRIG O' SPRING SOUP

1 can (10½ ounces) condensed
   cream of asparagus soup
1 soup can milk
¼ bunch watercress (about ¼ cup)
⅛ teaspoon basil
Dash pepper

Blend all ingredients 2 minutes in electric blender, or chop watercress very fine and combine with other ingredients in saucepan. Heat; stir now and then. Garnish with sprigs of watercress. 2 to 3 servings.

HOT BUTTERED SOUP

1 can (10½ ounces) condensed
   cream of asparagus soup
1 soup can water or milk
Butter

Combine soup and water. Heat; stir now and then. (If using milk, do not allow mixture to boil.) Pour into cups or mugs; garnish each with a pat of butter. 2 to 3 servings. Try a melt-in-your-soup butter pat atop celery, chicken, mushroom, tomato, and green pea soups, too, for extra cold or extra hungry soupsters.

BEEF BROTH WITH HORSERADISH

1 can (10½ ounces) condensed
   beef broth
1 cup water
½ teaspoon prepared horseradish
⅛ teaspoon dried dill leaves
Sour cream
Cucumber strips

Combine soup, water, horseradish, and dill. Simmer a few minutes. Pour into cups or mugs and top each serving with dab of sour cream. Use cucumber strips as crisp stirrers. 2 to 3 servings.

BEEF BROTH PLUS

1 can (10½ ounces) condensed
   beef broth
1 can (11¼ ounces) condensed
   green pea soup
1 can (10½ ounces) condensed
   tomato soup
1 soup can milk
1 tablespoon sherry (optional)
Crumbled bacon, if desired

Blend beef broth and green pea soups. Add tomato soup, milk, and sherry. Heat. Add a crunchy garnish of crumbled bacon. 4 to 6 servings.

TOMATO–VEGETABLE BEAN

1 can (10½ ounces) condensed
  tomato soup
1 can (10¾ ounces) condensed
  vegetable bean soup
1½ soup cans water

Combine soups and water. Heat; stir often. 4 servings.

VEGETABLE BROTH

1 can (10½ ounces) condensed
  beef broth
1 can (12 ounces) V-8
1 teaspoon lemon juice
⅛ teaspoon sweet basil, crushed

Combine beef broth, V-8, lemon juice, and basil. Simmer 1 or 2 minutes. 2 to 3 servings.

HAM 'N CHICKEN CHOWDER

½ cup cooked ham, cut in strips
1 tablespoon butter or margarine
1 can (10½ ounces) condensed
  cream of chicken soup
1 soup can water
½ cup cooked mixed vegetables

Cook ham in butter until lightly browned. Add remaining ingredients. Heat; stir often. 2 to 3 servings.

CHILLED TOMATO BOWL

1 can (10½ ounces) condensed
  consomme
1 can (10½ ounces) condensed
  tomato soup
½ soup can water
½ cup chopped cucumber
½ teaspoon dried chives, crushed
Dash "Tabasco" sauce
Sour cream, if desired

Blend soups and water; add cucumber, chives, and "Tabasco" sauce. Chill 4 hours. Serve with sour cream afloat. 4 generous servings.

BEEF NOODLE–VEGETABLE BEAN

1 can (10½ ounces) condensed beef
  noodle soup
1 can (10¾ ounces) condensed
  vegetable bean soup
1½ soup cans water

Combine soups and water. Heat; stir often. 4 servings.

CREAMY CHEESE BOWL

1 can (10½ ounces) condensed
   cream of chicken soup
1 soup can water
1 cup shredded mild process cheese
2 tablespoons sauterne or other dry
   white wine (optional)
⅛ teaspoon garlic powder

Combine all ingredients. Heat; stir often until cheese is melted. 2 to 3 servings.

CHICKEN SOUP AMANDINE

1 can (10½ ounces) condensed
   cream of chicken soup
1 soup can milk
¼ teaspoon grated onion
2 tablespoons chopped toasted
   almonds

Combine soup, milk, and onion. Heat. Garnish with almonds. 2 to 3 servings.

CURRIED CHICKEN SOUP

2 tablespoons chopped onion
1 tablespoon diced celery
1 to 2 teaspoons curry powder
1 tablespoon butter or margarine
1 can (10½ ounces) condensed
   cream of chicken soup
½ soup can milk
½ soup can water
Toasted almonds or coconut

In saucepan, cook onion and celery with curry powder in butter until tender. Blend in soup, milk, and water. Heat; stir now and then. Garnish with almonds or coconut. 2 to 3 servings.

GUMBO BOWL

1 can (10½ ounces) condensed
   chicken gumbo soup
½ soup can tomato juice
½ soup can water

Combine all ingredients. Heat; stir. 2 to 3 servings.

HERB CONSOMME

1 can (10½ ounces) condensed
   consomme
1 soup can water
Dash dill seed, tarragon, or basil

Combine all ingredients. Heat; simmer a few minutes. Garnish, if desired, with toast squares. 2 to 3 servings.

CURRIED COCONUT SHRIMP SOUP

2 teaspoons butter or margarine
¼ teaspoon curry powder
¼ cup flaked coconut
1 can (10 ounces) frozen condensed cream of shrimp soup
1 soup can milk

Melt butter in saucepan; stir in curry powder; add coconut; mix well. Cook and stir until lightly toasted. Remove from heat; set aside. Combine soup and milk. Heat until soup is thawed; stir now and then. Garnish each serving with curried coconut. 2 to 3 servings.

CLAMDIGGERS' CUP

2 cans (10½ ounces each) condensed tomato soup
1 cup clam juice
1 soup can water
¼ teaspoon leaf thyme, crushed

Combine all ingredients. Heat; stir. Serve in cups or mugs. 4 to 6 servings.

TANGY TOMATO SOUP

1 can (10½ ounces) condensed tomato soup
1 soup can water
½ teaspoon prepared horseradish
¼ teaspoon Worcestershire
Dash dry mustard

Combine all ingredients. Simmer 5 minutes; stir often. 2 to 3 servings.

BUTTERMILK BREW

1 can (10½ ounces) condensed tomato soup
1 cup water
⅓ cup buttermilk
¼ cup chopped cucumber
⅛ teaspoon dill seed

Combine all ingredients. Heat; *do not boil;* stir now and then. 2 to 3 servings.

EAST INDIA TOMATO SOUP

2 tablespoons thinly sliced green onion
1 tablespoon butter or margarine
1 can (10½ ounces) condensed tomato soup
1 soup can water
¼ teaspoon curry powder

Cook green onion in butter until lightly browned. Add soup, water, and curry powder. Heat; stir. Serve hot or chill at least 4 hours and serve. 2 to 3 servings.

HEARTY BEEF WARM-UP

½ cup sliced mushrooms
1 small green pepper, sliced
1 tablespoon butter or margarine
1 can (10½ ounces) condensed
   beef noodle soup
1 can (10¾ ounces) condensed
   beef soup
1½ soup cans water

Cook mushrooms and green pepper in butter until tender. Add soups and water. Heat. 4 servings.

CHRISTMAS NOODLE CUP

1 can (10½ ounces) condensed
   beef noodle soup
1 soup can water
1 teaspoon finely chopped parsley
1 teaspoon chopped pimiento

Combine all ingredients. Heat; stir often. Garnish with wreath of chopped parsley or red bell cut from pimiento. 2 to 3 servings.

BLACK BEAN FLOAT

1 can (10½ ounces) condensed
   black bean soup
1 soup can water
½ teaspoon minced instant onion
½ teaspoon lemon juice
¼ cup sour cream
1½ teaspoons chopped parsley
1½ teaspoons chopped radish

Combine soup, water, onion, and lemon juice. Heat; stir now and then. Meanwhile, combine sour cream, parsley, and radish; float on soup as a bright, contrasting garnish. 2 to 3 servings.

CELERY-CLOVE COMBO

1 can (10½ ounces) condensed
   cream of celery soup
1 can (10½ ounces) condensed
   tomato soup
1 cup water
1 cup milk
Dash ground cloves
Chopped toasted almonds, if desired

Blend soups, water, milk, and cloves. Heat; stir now and then until "serving hot", then sprinkle each serving with chopped almonds. 4 servings.

V-8 VEGETABLE POTAGE

1 can (10¾ ounces) condensed
   vegetable soup
½ soup can "V-8" juice
½ soup can water

Combine all ingredients. Heat. Garnish with popcorn, if desired. 2 to 3 servings.

CREME CELERY-TOMATO

1 can (10½ ounces) condensed
   cream of celery soup
1 soup can water
½ cup chopped tomato
2 tablespoons chopped green onion
2 tablespoons chopped green
   pepper
¼ cup sour cream

Combine all ingredients; chill. Serve in chilled bowls. 3 to 4 servings.

COUNTRY FAIR SOUP

¼ cup diced cooked ham
1 tablespoon butter or margarine
Dash ground marjoram, if desired
1 can (10¾ ounces) condensed
   turkey vegetable soup
1 soup can water

Brown ham in butter with marjoram. Add soup and water. Heat. 2 to 3 servings.

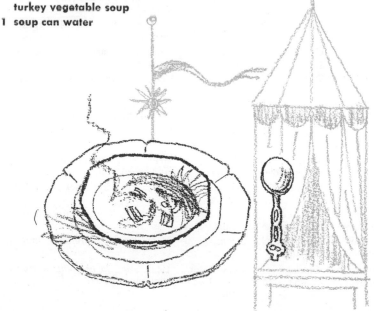

MIX-MATCH SOUPS AND SERVE AS SOUP MATES

One soup	+Second soup	+Liquid	=Soup Mate
Cream of Asparagus	Cream of Chicken	1½ cans milk or water	Heat, stir; *do not boil.* Garnish with shreds of orange peel.
Cream of Asparagus	Scotch Broth	1½ cans water	Heat, stir. New lunch flavor.
Bean with Bacon	Minestrone	2 cans water	Heat, stir. Pass hot French rolls.
Bean with Bacon	Vegetable	1½ cans water	Heat, stir. Ladle from bean pot.
Beef	Pepper Pot	2 cans water	Heat, stir. Dot with popcorn.
Beef	Tomato	2 cans water	Heat, stir. Add 1 teaspoon sherry, if desired. Top with chopped parsley or chives.
Beef	Tomato Rice	1½ cans water	Heat, stir. Winter picnic warmup.
Beef Broth	Beef Noodle	1½ cans water	Heat, stir. Topping of herb-seasoned stuffing.
Beef Broth	Tomato	1½ cans water	Heat, stir. Float toast squares on top.
Beef Noodle	Minestrone	2 cans water	Heat, stir. Schoolboy's lunch in vacuum.
Beef Noodle	Tomato	1½ cans water	Heat, stir. Ladle from bright casserole.
Beef Noodle	Vegetable Beef	1½ cans water	Heat, stir. Sprinkle with grated cheese.
Black Bean	Consommé	1½ cans water	Heat, stir. Garnish with lemon slices.
Cheddar Cheese	Tomato	1½ to 2 cans water	Heat, stir; *do not boil.* Elegant in chowder mugs.
Chicken & Stars	Chicken Noodle	2 cans water	Heat. This makes "Stars and Stripes" for patriotic party themes.
Chicken Gumbo	Tomato	1½ to 2 cans water	Heat, stir. Perfect party appetizer.
Chicken Noodle	Vegetarian Vegetable	1½ cans water	Heat, stir. Accompaniment to cold sliced beef.
Chicken with Rice	Tomato	1½ cans water	Heat, stir. China soup cups on silver tray.
Chicken Vegetable	Cream of Vegetable	1½ to 2 cans water	Heat, stir. Cheese cubes afloat.
Chili Beef	Vegetable Beef	2 cans water	Heat, stir. Pass "Goldfish" crackers.
Cream of Celery	Chicken Vegetable	1 can water and 1 can milk	Heat, stir; *do not boil.* Stirrers: cucumber spears.

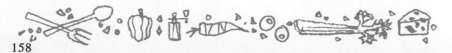

MIX-MATCH SOUPS AND SERVE AS SOUP MATES

One soup	+Second soup	+Liquid	=Soup Mate
Cream of Celery	Vegetarian Vegetable	1½ cans water	Heat, stir. Good with grilled cheese sandwich.
Cream of Chicken	Chicken Gumbo	2 cans water or milk	Heat, stir; *do not boil if milk used.* Add dash of curry or coconut, if desired.
Cream of Chicken	Chicken with Rice	1½ to 2 cans water or milk	Heat, stir; *do not boil if milk used.* Break in breakfast routine; top with crisp cereal.
Cream of Mushroom	Cream of Asparagus	2 cans milk, or 1 can milk and 1 can water	Stir mushroom soup to smooth. Blend in asparagus soup and liquid. Heat; *do not boil.* Top with watercress.
Cream of Mushroom	Chicken with Rice	1½ cans water	Stir mushroom soup to smooth. Blend in other soup and liquid. Heat; *do not boil.* Form family "soup line".
Cream of Mushroom	Consommé	1½ cans water	Stir mushroom soup to smooth. Blend in other soup and liquid. Heat; *do not boil.* Top with toasted almonds.
Clam Chowder (Manhattan Style)	Green Pea	2 cans water	Heat, stir. Serve with garnish of sieved egg yolk.
Consommé	Scotch Broth	1½ cans water	Heat, stir; *do not boil.* Cheese crackers to munch.
Consommé	Bisque of Tomato	1½ cans water	Mix and heat. Garnish with sour cream.
Green Pea	Scotch Broth	1½ cans water	Heat, stir. Serve with party rye slices.
Noodles & Ground Beef	Old Fashioned Vegetable	2 cans water	Heat this hearty combination to enjoy with egg salad sandwich.
Pepper Pot	Vegetable Beef	2 cans water	Heat, stir. Savor at Saturday lunch.
Turkey Noodle	Vegetable	1½ cans water	Heat, stir. Keep warm in chafing dish or electric kettle.

Great Soups

Almost every country has a great soup that uses the best of its lands and seas.

In French port towns, bouillabaisse holds the best of the seafood catch; in French farm country, the green pea and onion contribute to distinctive potages. In Scotland, barley goes into the broth; in India, curry flavors soup.

In Maryland, U.S.A., the crab makes a great bisque; in New England, clam is the chowder choice. Everywhere, U.S.A., the ruddy farm tomato becomes the nation's favorite soup.

How did great soups win their claim to fame? There is much food history on this fascinating subject. For example, back in the twelfth century, soup-making became such an art that sometimes five or six kinds were served at a single meal!

A famous restaurant of long ago served only soup. The year was 1765, the place Paris. An enterprising tradesman, Monsieur Boulanger, offered what he called "restaurantes" or pickups—bowls of soup which could be bought at any hour. His soups were so popular, other people copied the custom, and eventually other prepared dishes were offered as well. With canned soups handy, you can offer "restaurantes" at any hour, too.

Let great soups from around the world be part of your family meals. Have fun cooking these modern versions.

CLAM CHOWDER

Clam chowder, named for the French *chaudier* in which it was cooked in Brittany, is canned now in creamy New England style as well as rosy Manhattan variety with tomatoes and other vegetables . . . and never the partisans of each shall meet. Both appetites can be readily satisfied. Prepared chowders are quick to heat and serve, making, as an old recipe puts it, "a dish fit for the best of the nation".

MULLIGATAWNY SOUP

Mulligatawny means "Pepper water" in India, a curry-flavored soup.

2 cans (10½ ounces each) condensed cream of chicken soup
1 can (10½ ounces) condensed chicken with rice soup
1½ soup cans water
½ to 1 teaspoon curry powder

Blend soups, water, and curry powder. Heat; stir occasionally. 6 servings.

QUICK MOCK BOUILLABAISSE

Streamlined version of the fish stew native to Marseilles.

1 small onion, sliced
1 small clove garlic, minced
½ small bay leaf
¼ teaspoon thyme, crushed
2 tablespoons olive oil
1 can (10½ ounces) condensed tomato soup
1 soup can water
2 cups cooked seafood (crab, fish, lobster, shrimp)
1 teaspoon lemon juice
Dash "Tabasco" sauce
4 slices French bread, toasted

Cook onion, garlic, bay leaf, and thyme in olive oil until onion is tender. Add soup, water, seafood (any combination you like), lemon juice, and "Tabasco" sauce. Bring to boil. Cover; simmer 5 minutes. To serve: ladle soup over toast in bowls. 3 to 4 servings.

LOBSTER BISQUE

Bisques are often smooth and creamy, flavored with shellfish.

2 tablespoons chopped celery
½ teaspoon curry powder
1 tablespoon butter or margarine
1 can (10 ounces) frozen condensed cream of shrimp soup
1 soup can water
1 cup diced cooked lobster

In saucepan, cook celery and curry in butter until tender. Add soup, water, and lobster. Heat; stir now and then. Do not boil. 2 to 3 servings.

CIOPPINO

Glorified fish soup, a specialty at California's Fisherman's Wharf.

½ cup chopped green pepper
½ cup chopped onion
2 tablespoons chopped parsley
2 cloves garlic, minced
¼ cup olive oil
2 cans (10½ ounces each) condensed tomato soup
1 soup can water
¼ teaspoon basil, crushed
1 bay leaf
¼ teaspoon grated lemon rind
⅛ teaspoon salt
Dash pepper
¼ cup dry white wine (optional)
1 pound haddock fillets, cut in 2-inch pieces
1 pound fresh shrimp, shelled
½ pound cooked crab meat

Cook green pepper, onion, parsley, and garlic in olive oil until vegetables are tender. Stir in soup, water, basil, bay leaf, lemon rind, salt, and pepper. Cook over low heat about 10 minutes to blend flavors. Add remaining ingredients. Cook 10 minutes more. Stir gently now and then. 6 to 8 servings.

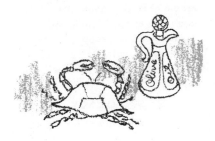

MARYLAND BISQUE

A Peninsula blend of seafood flavors you can make quickly.

2 cups diced raw potatoes
2 cups water
1 can (10 ounces) frozen condensed oyster stew
1 can (10 ounces) frozen condensed cream of shrimp soup
2 tablespoons chopped parsley

In covered saucepan, cook potatoes in water until done. Add soups and parsley. Heat until thawed; stir often. 4 to 6 servings.

YANKEE CHOWDER

A hearty, rugged inland blend of what's handy for the big soup pot.

1 can (10½ ounces) condensed cream of mushroom soup
3 soup cans water
1 can (10½ ounces) condensed turkey noodle soup
1 can (10½ ounces) condensed vegetarian vegetable soup

Stir mushroom soup until smooth in large saucepan; gradually blend in water. Add remaining soups. Heat thoroughly; stir often. 6 to 8 servings.

CHICKEN CHOWDER

Potatoes and chicken in a creamy blend, Massachusetts farm choice.

½ cup chopped celery
1 tablespoon butter or margarine
1 can (10¼ ounces) frozen condensed cream of potato soup
1 soup can water or milk
1 can (5 ounces) boned chicken or turkey, or 1 cup diced cooked chicken or turkey
1 tablespoon minced parsley

In covered saucepan, cook celery in butter over very low heat until tender but not browned. Add soup and water. Heat until soup is thawed; stir often. Add contents of can of chicken and parsley. Simmer to blend flavors. 3 to 4 servings.

GUMBO

New Orleans soup with shrimp and ham.

½ cup diced cooked ham
¼ cup chopped celery with leaves
¼ cup chopped green pepper
¼ cup chopped onion
Generous dash leaf thyme
2 tablespoons butter or margarine
2 cans (10½ ounces each) condensed chicken gumbo soup
2 soup cans water
1 cup cooked shrimp (about ½ pound uncooked)

Cook ham, celery, green pepper, onion, and thyme in butter until vegetables are tender and ham is browned. Add remaining ingredients. Cook over low heat a few minutes; stir now and then. 6 to 8 servings.

GREEK LEMON SOUP

"Soup Avgolemo" to the Greeks, this has rare delicate tang.

1 can (10½ ounces) condensed chicken with rice soup
1 soup can water
1 egg
2 teaspoons lemon juice
Nutmeg
Butter

Blend soup and water; heat. Meanwhile, beat egg and lemon juice together in small bowl until well blended. Add a little hot soup to egg mixture; stir constantly. Remove remaining soup from heat; slowly stir in egg mixture (this method prevents curdling). Serve immediately. Garnish with nutmeg or butter, if desired. 2 to 3 servings.

MARDI GRAS GUMBO

Okra, crab, and rice in a flavorful base, gay as the Mardi Gras!

1 can (10½ ounces) condensed
   chicken gumbo soup
1 can (10½ ounces) condensed
   tomato soup
1½ soup cans water
1 can (7 ounces) crab, flaked
2 tablespoons sherry (optional)
2 cups cooked rice

Combine ingredients, except rice. Heat; stir now and then. To serve, line a large bowl or tureen with the cooked rice and pour in the soup. 6 to 8 servings.

WILLIAMSBURG PUMPKIN SOUP

Pumpkin purée blends with creamy chicken, a Colonial discovery.

¼ cup finely chopped onion
2 tablespoons butter or margarine
1 can (10½ ounces) condensed
   cream of chicken soup
1 soup can water
½ cup canned or mashed cooked
   pumpkin
Dash ground nutmeg
Dash pepper

Cook onion in butter until tender Add soup and remaining ingredients. Heat; stir often. 2 to 3 servings. (Can be served with croutons.)

POLISH CABBAGE SOUP

A Balkan stew-soup to make a supper.

¾ pound lean pork, cut in small
   pieces
1 tablespoon butter or margarine
1 can (10½ ounces) condensed
   beef broth
1 can (10½ ounces) condensed
   tomato soup
2 soup cans water
4 cups shredded cabbage (about 1
   pound)
½ cup chopped onion
2 teaspoons salt
½ teaspoon paprika
1 bay leaf
Dash pepper
1 tablespoon sherry (optional)
Sour cream

Brown pork in butter. Add remaining ingredients except sour cream. Cover; cook over low heat 30 minutes; stir often. Serve with spoonsful of sour cream. 6 servings.

164

COCK-A-LEEKIE

Scottish wives simmer chicken with leeks and vegetables, serve soup one day,
chicken the next. The prunes—a tasty tradition.

2 leeks, thinly sliced
2 tablespoons butter or margarine
2 cans (10¾ ounces each) condensed chicken vegetable soup
2 soup cans water
4 to 6 cooked prunes (pitted), if desired
½ teaspoon salt
Dash pepper

Cook leeks in butter until tender. Add remaining ingredients. Heat; stir now and then. 4 to 6 servings.

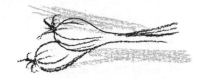

GOULASH SOUP

1 cup cubed cooked beef
¼ cup chopped green pepper
½ teaspoon paprika
2 tablespoons butter or margarine
1 can (10¾ ounces) condensed tomato soup
1 soup can water
½ teaspoon caraway seed

In saucepan, brown beef and cook green pepper and paprika in butter until green pepper is tender. Add remaining ingredients. Heat; stir now and then. 3 servings.

GREEN AND YELLOW SOUP

⅓ cup grated cabbage
⅓ cup grated carrot
¼ cup chopped onion
2 tablespoons butter or margarine
1 can (10½ ounces) frozen condensed green pea with ham soup
1 soup can water
1 tablespoon sauterne (optional)

Cook cabbage, carrot, and onion in butter until tender. Add remaining ingredients; heat. Stir now and then. 2 to 3 servings.

POTAGE ST. GERMAIN

This tangy pea soup with chicken is justly famed in France.

1 can (10½ ounces) condensed cream of chicken soup
1 can (11¼ ounces) condensed green pea soup
2 cups milk
½ cup heavy cream
½ cup cooked sliced carrot

Stir soups, milk, and cream until smooth. Add carrot. Heat; stir often. 4 to 6 servings.

PURÉE MONGOLE

A purée is sieved—but you need no strainer for this combination.

1 can (11¼ ounces) condensed green pea soup
1 can (10½ ounces) condensed tomato soup
1 cup milk
1 cup water

Blend soups, milk, and water in saucepan. Heat; *but do not boil.* Add a dash of curry powder, if desired. 4 to 5 servings.

CHINESE SWEET AND SOUR SOUP

Tender chicken pieces in broth with Oriental seasoning.

1 raw chicken breast (½ pound)
¼ teaspoon salt
1 tablespoon cornstarch
3 tablespoons water
1 tablespoon soy sauce
2 cans (10½ ounces each) condensed beef broth
1 soup can water
1 can (4 ounces) sliced mushrooms and liquid
2 tablespoons vinegar
1 tablespoon sugar
Lemon slices

Skin chicken with sharp knife; cut into thin 2-inch long slices. Sprinkle with salt. Mix cornstarch with 3 tablespoons water and soy sauce; combine with beef broth and water. Bring to boil; stir often; add chicken, mushrooms and liquid, vinegar, and sugar. Heat. Simmer 5 minutes. Serve with a slice of lemon in each bowl, a cruet of vinegar on the table. 4 to 6 servings.

MEXICAN FOAM SOUP

¼ cup chopped onion
2 tablespoons chopped green pepper
1 tablespoon butter or margarine
1 can (10½ ounces) condensed tomato soup
1 soup can milk
Generous dash red pepper
1 egg, separated

Cook onion and green pepper in butter until tender. Stir in soup, milk, and red pepper. Heat; *but do not boil.* Slightly beat egg yolk; stir a little hot soup into yolk; gradually add to soup. Beat egg white until very soft peaks form; add ½ cup soup mixture; beat lightly. Pour on top of soup; heat. 2 to 3 servings.

Barbecued Steak Supreme   Page 24
Divan Sandwich   Page 119
Peppy Burger   Page 116

BORSCHT

There is rare color and flavor in the bright Russian peasant soup.

2 cups shredded fresh beets
1 tablespoon butter or margarine
1 tablespoon vinegar or lemon juice
2 cans (10½ ounces each) condensed consomme
1 can (10½ ounces) condensed onion soup
1 soup can water
½ cup tomato juice
2 cups shredded cabbage
¼ to ½ cup sour cream

Cook beets in butter a few minutes. Add vinegar. Cover. Cook over very low heat 20 minutes. Add soups, water, tomato juice, and cabbage. Cover. Cook 10 minutes more or until vegetables are tender. Serve with sour cream (as a garnish or stirred in just before serving). May also be served cold. 5 to 6 servings.

NOTE: If desired, 1 can (1 pound) beets may be used in place of fresh beets. Chop beets; cook in butter a few minutes. Add remaining ingredients (using liquid from beets plus water, to make 1 cup, in place of water in above recipe). Cover and simmer 10 minutes. Serve with sour cream.

FRENCH ONION SOUP

1 can (10½ ounces) condensed onion soup
1 soup can water
2 or 3 slices French or Italian bread (about ½-inch thick)
Butter
Grated Parmesan cheese

Combine soup and water. Heat; let simmer a few minutes. Meanwhile, arrange bread on cookie sheet; spread with butter and sprinkle with Parmesan cheese. Broil until lightly browned. Pour soup into bowls; top each with a cheese crouton. 2 to 3 servings.

GREEN PEA FRANCAIS

In 17th Century France, peas were the food of kings . . . kingly still.

1 can (2 ounces) mushroom stems and pieces
1 tablespoon butter or margarine
2 cans (11¼ ounces each) condensed green pea soup
2 soup cans water and mushroom liquid
1 cup grated carrot

Drain mushrooms, saving liquid. Saute in butter. Add soup, water, and mushroom liquid; stir until smooth. Add carrot. Heat; simmer 10 minutes or until carrot is tender and flavors blended. 4 to 6 servings.

Chicken Noodle Soup, Vichysoisse Page 179, Minestrone
Tomato Soup with Popcorn, Vegetable Soup, Jellied Consomme with Lemon Slice
Chicken Vegetable Soup, Green Pea with Ham Soup Topped with Cereal Bits, French Onion Soup with Parmesan Crouton   Page 169

SENEGALESE SOUP

Curry and chicken have an affinity in the soup bowl, too.

1 can (10½ ounces) condensed
cream of chicken soup
⅛ teaspoon curry powder
1 soup can milk

Stir soup; blend in curry powder. Add milk gradually. Place in refrigerator for at least 4 hours. Serve in chilled bowls. 2 to 3 servings.

VATAPA

Unusual South American blend of broth, shellfish, nuts.

1 can (10½ ounces) condensed
beef broth
2 cans (10¾ ounces each) condensed
clam chowder (Manhattan style)
2 soup cans water
½ cup chopped salted peanuts
¼ cup tender-thin flaked coconut
1 bay leaf
Few drops "Tabasco" sauce
1 pound shrimp, peeled and
deveined

Combine all ingredients except shrimp; cover and bring to boil; stir often. Add shrimp; simmer 5 minutes or until tender. Remove bay leaf before serving. 8 servings.

LOBSTER CHOWDER

¼ cup chopped onion
2 tablespoons butter or margarine
2 cans (11 ounces each) condensed
Cheddar cheese soup
1 soup can milk
1 soup can water
1 cup flaked cooked lobster
2 tablespoons chopped parsley
Dash pepper
Dash paprika

Cook onion in butter until tender. Stir in soup until smooth; gradually blend in milk and water. Add lobster, parsley, and pepper. Heat; stir often. Garnish with paprika. 4 to 6 servings.

TURKEY VEGETABLE CUP

1 can (2 ounces) mushroom stems
and pieces, drained
1 tablespoon butter or margarine
Dash leaf thyme, crushed
1 can (10¾ ounces) condensed
turkey vegetable soup
1 soup can water

Brown mushrooms in butter with thyme. Stir in soup and water. Heat. 2 to 3 servings.
VARIATION: Substitute ¼ cup diced chopped ham for mushrooms and dash ground marjoram for thyme, if desired.

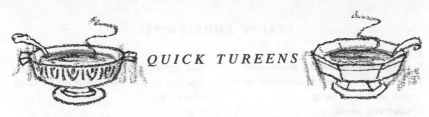

QUICK TUREENS

A new group of great soups takes high honors these days. Subtle flavor-blends challenge the great soups of the past. These are quickly created by combining canned soups in generous proportions and adding accents of other foods for tantalizing flavor.

MAINE FISH SOUP

½ cup chopped onion
1 tablespoon butter or margarine
1 can (10½ ounces) condensed cream of celery soup
1 can (10¾ ounces) condensed clam chowder (Manhattan style)
1½ soup cans water
1 cup flaked cooked white fish or tuna (7-ounce can, drained and flaked) or shrimp (6-ounce can, drained)
1 tablespoon chopped parsley

Cook onion in butter until tender. Blend in remaining ingredients. Simmer a few minutes; stir often. 6 servings.

BEANESTRONE

1 cup diced cooked ham
2 tablespoons chopped onion
1 tablespoon butter or margarine
1 can (11¼ ounces) condensed bean with bacon soup
2 soup cans water
1 can (10¾ ounces) condensed minestrone soup

Brown ham and onion in butter. Stir in bean with bacon soup; blend in water. Add minestrone soup. Heat; stir often. 4 to 6 servings.

MEATBALL SOUP

½ pound ground beef, seasoned
1 can (11¼ ounces) condensed bean with bacon, cream of vegetable, celery, mushroom, green pea, minestrone, onion, tomato, or vegetable soup
1 soup can water

Shape meat into 8 small meatballs; brown slowly in saucepan. (Use a little shortening if necessary.) Pour off any excess drippings. Stir in soup and water; simmer a few minutes. 2 to 3 servings.

SPRING SOUP BOWL

2 tablespoons chopped onion
1 tablespoon butter or margarine
1 can (11¼ ounces) condensed split
    pea with ham soup
1 soup can water
2 tablespoons chopped pimiento

Cook onion in butter until tender. Add soup; gradually stir in water. Add pimiento. Heat; stir often. 2 to 3 servings.

COUNTRY FAVORITE

2 slices bacon
2 tablespoons chopped onion
⅛ teaspoon leaf thyme, crushed
1 can (10¾ ounces) condensed
    vegetable bean soup
1 soup can water
½ cup cooked cut green beans

Cook bacon until crisp; remove and crumble. Pour off all but 1 tablespoon drippings. Add onion and thyme; cook until onion is tender. Add soup, water, and beans. Heat; stir often. Top each serving with bacon. 3 servings.

VEGETABLE BEAN FRANKFURTER SOUP

1 frankfurter, thinly sliced
2 tablespoons chopped onion
1 tablespoon butter or margarine
1 can (10¾ ounces) condensed
    vegetable bean soup
1 soup can water

Brown frankfurter slices and onion in butter. Stir in soup and water. Heat; stir often. 2 to 3 servings.

CANADIAN COUNTRY SOUP

4 ounces sliced Canadian bacon, cut
    into small pieces
½ cup chopped onion
1 tablespoon butter or margarine
1 can (11¼ ounces) condensed bean
    with bacon soup
1 can (10½ ounces) condensed
    cream of mushroom soup
1 can (10½ ounces) condensed
    vegetarian vegetable soup
2 soup cans water
1 cup drained cooked whole kernel
    corn

Brown bacon and cook onion in butter until tender. Blend in soups and water; add corn. Heat; stir often. 6 to 8 servings.

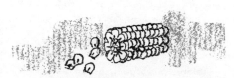

172

SOUTHERN BEEF SOUP

1 jar (2½ ounces) sliced dried beef, cut into small pieces
¼ cup chopped onion
2 tablespoons butter or margarine
1 can (10½ ounces) condensed cream of celery soup
1 can (10½ ounces) condensed cream of mushroom soup
1 soup can water
½ soup can milk
1 cup cooked succotash
½ cup cooked tomatoes

Pour boiling water over beef; drain. In saucepan, cook beef and onion in butter until onion is tender. Add soups; stir until smooth. Add remaining ingredients. Heat; stir often. 4 servings.

CRAB BISQUE

¼ cup chopped onion
⅛ teaspoon leaf thyme
1 tablespoon butter or margarine
1 can (10¾ ounces) condensed cream of vegetable soup
½ soup can milk
½ soup can water
1 cup flaked cooked crab (or 7-ounce can, drained)
¼ cup chopped cooked broccoli
Lemon wedges

Cook onion and thyme in butter until onion is tender. Add remaining ingredients except lemon wedges. Heat; stir often. Serve with lemon wedges. 3 to 4 servings.

CELERY TURKEY TUREEN

¼ cup chopped onion
1 tablespoon butter or margarine
1 can (10½ ounces) condensed cream of celery soup
1 can (10½ ounces) condensed turkey noodle soup
1 cup milk
1 cup water
1 cup cream-style corn
Chopped parsley

Cook onion slowly in butter until tender but not browned. Blend in soups, milk, and water; add corn. Heat; stir often. Serve with a garnish of chopped parsley. 4 to 6 servings.

CHICKEN MUSHROOM POTAGE

1 can (10½ ounces) condensed
  cream of mushroom soup
1 can (10¾ ounces) condensed
  chicken vegetable soup
1½ soup cans water
1 cup chopped fresh spinach
1 cup diced cooked ham
Dash allspice
Dash mace

Stir cream of mushroom soup until
smooth. Add remaining ingredients.
Heat; stir often. 4 to 6 servings.

CHICKEN CANJA

½ cup diced cooked ham
1 tablespoon butter or margarine
1 can (10½ ounces) condensed
  cream of chicken soup
1 can (10¾ ounces) condensed
  chicken vegetable soup
2 soup cans water
1 tablespoon chopped parsley

Lightly brown ham in butter. Blend
in soups, water, and parsley. Heat;
stir often. 4 to 6 servings.

SHRIMP-POTATO SOUP

1 can (10¼ ounces) frozen condensed cream of potato soup
1 can (10 ounces) frozen condensed
  cream of shrimp soup
1 cup milk
1 cup water
½ cup cooked whole kernel corn
1 tablespoon chopped parsley
4 drops "Tabasco" sauce

Combine all ingredients. Heat until
soups are thawed; stir often. 4 to 5
servings.

TUNA VEGETABLE BOWL

2 tablespoons chopped onion
2 tablespoons chopped parsley
Dash leaf thyme
2 tablespoons butter or margarine
1 can (10¾ ounces) condensed
  cream of vegetable soup
½ soup can milk
½ soup can water
1 can (7 ounces) tuna, drained
  and flaked

Cook onion, parsley, and thyme in
butter until onion is tender. Blend
in soup, milk, and water. Add tuna.
Heat; stir often. 3 servings.

Frosty Soups

Count three special appeals for cold summer soups. They are taste-tantalizing appetizers, as in creamy smooth Vichyssoise, or shimmering jellied consomme. They make refreshing pickups to sip when you want to feel cooler. They look inviting, set out on the table in ice-lined bowls, or garnished with fresh vegetables.

Cold soups were made fashionable back in the seventeenth century by Louis XIV—for a very practical reason. Each of the king's dishes was tasted by several people before it came to him. The monarch grew tired of lukewarm soup, and requested tasty cold soups, instead.

Twentieth-century chef Louis Diat invented one of the most famous frosty soups, Vichyssoise, at the Ritz-Carlton in New York City—and what a success it was! Now you can try Vichyssoise in at least four quick versions, or add your own to this chapter of cold summer soups.

QUICK METHOD

Keep cans of your favorite soup in refrigerator. Combine with other chilled ingredients to eliminate chilling time. Quick dishes for gourmet fare.

AVOCADO CHICKEN BOWL

1 can (10½ ounces) condensed
  cream of chicken soup
1 soup can milk
½ cup chopped celery
1 to 2 tablespoons chopped onion
1 ripe avocado, mashed

In blender, combine all ingredients except avocado; blend until smooth. Chill at least 4 hours. Add avocado; blend until smooth. Thin to desired consistency with milk. Serve immediately in chilled bowls. 3 to 4 servings.

BLACK FROST

1 can (10½ ounces) condensed black
  bean soup
1 can (10½ ounces) condensed
  consomme
1 soup can water
1 to 2 teaspoons sherry (optional)
Lemon slices

Stir black bean soup well; add consomme, water, and sherry. Heat; stir now and then. Chill 4 hours. Serve in icy cold bowls. Garnish each serving with a lemon slice. 4 servings.

CRAB BOWL

1 can (10½ ounces) condensed
  cream of celery soup
1 soup can water
½ cup flaked cooked crab
1 tablespoon thinly sliced green
  onion
½ medium tomato, cut in cubes
¼ teaspoon grated lemon rind
Lemon wedges

Blend soup and water; stir in crab, onion, tomato, and lemon rind. Place in refrigerator for at least 4 hours. Serve in chilled bowls; garnish with lemon wedges. 2 to 3 servings.

DUTCH POTAGE

1 can (10¼ ounces) frozen condensed cream of potato soup
1 soup can water
⅛ teaspoon caraway seed
¼ cup sour cream
½ cup shredded cabbage
2 tablespoons shredded carrot
1 tablespoon chopped green pepper

Combine soup, water, and caraway seed. Heat until soup is thawed; stir often. Blend in sour cream and remaining ingredients. Place in refrigerator for about 4 hours. Serve in chilled bowls. If desired, thin with milk before serving. 3 to 4 servings.

CUCUMBER COOLER

1 can (10½ ounces) condensed
  cream of celery soup
1 cup milk
1 small cucumber, diced (about 1
  cup)
Dash "Tabasco" sauce
Dash salt and pepper
1 cup sour cream

Combine soup, milk, cucumber, "Tabasco" sauce, and seasonings in electric blender; blend for 2 minutes. Stir in sour cream. Place in refrigerator for at least 4 hours. Serve in chilled bowls. 3 to 4 servings.

JELLIED SOUP-SALAD

2 cans (10½ ounces each) condensed
consomme
¼ cup diced green pepper
2 tablespoons chopped parsley
1 tablespoon minced onion
1 tablespoon butter or margarine
½ teaspoon curry powder
¼ cup slivered blanched almonds
Dash salt

Combine consomme, green pepper, parsley, and onion. Chill until jellied—about 4 hours. Stir when partially jellied to distribute vegetables. Melt butter in a small frying pan; add curry powder, almonds, and salt. Cook over low heat, until lightly browned; drain. Serve consomme in chilled bowls; top with almonds. 4 servings.

LOBSTER POT

2 cans (10½ ounces each) condensed consomme
1 can (6 ounces) lobster, drained
and flaked
½ cup cubed avocado
¼ cup chopped celery
2 tablespoons chopped green onion
2 tablespoons lemon juice
Dash "Tabasco" sauce
Dash pepper

Combine consomme with other ingredients. Chill until jellied—about 4 hours. Stir when partially jellied to distribute lobster and vegetables. Serve with lemon wedges, if desired. 4 to 6 servings.

GAZPACHO

1 can (10¾ ounces) condensed
tomato soup
1 cup water
1 tablespoon olive oil
2 tablespoons wine vinegar
1 large clove garlic, minced
1 cup finely chopped cucumber
½ cup finely chopped green pepper
¼ cup finely chopped onion

In bowl, combine soup, water, oil, vinegar, and garlic. Chill 4 hours. Serve in chilled bowls. Pass chilled vegetables for garnishes (also croutons if desired). 3 servings.

PARFAIT CONSOMME

1 can (10½ ounces) condensed
consomme
½ cup sour cream
2 tablespoons chopped chives

Place unopened can of consomme in refrigerator until jellied, about 4 hours. To serve, spoon a little consomme into each parfait glass; top with sour cream. Repeat layers; sprinkle chives on top. 2 to 3 servings.

SOUP-ON-THE-ROCKS

The easiest and most popular of frosted soups is yours to enjoy anywhere. Simply fill a broad glass with ice cubes. Pour beef broth, right from the can, over the cubes. Garnish with a slice or wedge of lemon or lime. NOTE: For variety add a fleck of spice to the beef broth before pouring over ice cubes, perhaps curry, nutmeg, cinnamon, allspice, or ginger.

WHITE MOUNTAIN REFRESHER

1 can (10¼ ounces) frozen condensed cream of potato soup
1 soup can water
½ cup sour cream
¼ cup finely chopped cucumber

Combine soup and water. Heat slowly until soup is thawed; stir now and then. Beat until smooth with electric blender or rotary beater. Blend in sour cream and cucumber. Place in refrigerator for at least 4 hours. Serve in well-chilled bowls. 3 servings.

SHRIMP GLACÉ

1 can (10 ounces) frozen condensed cream of shrimp soup
1 soup can water
1 cup chopped fresh spinach
¼ cup chopped celery
½ teaspoon grated lemon rind

Combine soup and water. Heat until soup is thawed; stir often. Add remaining ingredients. Place in refrigerator at least 4 hours. Serve in chilled bowls. 3 servings.

GARNISHES: Top with choice of chopped watercress, stuffed olive slices, minced parsley, snipped chives, radish slices, or slivered toasted almonds.

VICHYSSOISE

1 can (10¼ ounces) frozen condensed cream of potato soup
½ soup can milk
½ soup can light cream

Heat soup, milk, and cream over low heat until soup is completely thawed; stir now and then. Beat until smooth in an electric mixer or blender. Place in refrigerator for at least 4 hours. Serve in chilled bowls. 3 servings.

QUICK METHOD: Place unopened can of soup in pan of hot water for 30 minutes to thaw. In electric blender, combine soup and 1 soup can milk; beat *just* until smooth. Serve immediately in chilled bowls or place in refrigerator until ready to serve.

GARNISHES: minced chives, minced green pepper, minced parsley, shredded process or grated Parmesan cheese, shredded beets, sliced stuffed olives, minced celery, thinly sliced radishes, chopped cucumber, shredded carrot.

FLORENTINE VICHYSSOISE

1 can (10¼ ounces) frozen condensed cream of potato soup
1 soup can water or milk
1 cup finely chopped fresh spinach
(or ¼ cup cooked spinach)

Combine soup, liquid, and spinach. (If using cooked spinach, add to soup when it thaws.) Cover. Heat slowly until thawed. Stir now and then. Serve hot or chill 4 hours before serving. If desired, pour into blender and blend until smooth. 3 servings.

PINK VICHYSSOISE

1 can (10¼ ounces) frozen condensed cream of potato soup,
thawed
½ soup can light cream
1 cup chilled tomato juice

In electric mixer or blender, combine soup, cream, and tomato juice. Beat until smooth. Serve immediately in chilled bowls. 3 to 4 servings.

Dress-Up
Garnishes

"Only the pure in heart can make a good soup" Beethoven wrote. The artistic can dress it up, he might have added. When soup comes to the table—hot or cold, thick or clear—a bit of contrast in texture, color, or flavor sets it off to appetizing advantage.

Achieve soup distinctiveness through garnishes such as these which are good on most any soup: chopped parsley, watercress, or chives—thin-sliced lemon or grated rind—sliced cooked mushrooms—sour cream or salted whipped cream—packaged stuffing—toasted nuts—sliced green onions—chopped ripe olives—crisp bacon—potato chips and corn chips—crisp cereal.

Many recipes follow for other ideas.

ZESTY PAN-TOASTED CRACKERS

1 cup oyster crackers
1 tablespoon butter, melted
Celery or onion salt

Add crackers to butter; heat. Shake pan to coat crackers with butter. Sprinkle with celery or onion salt. Especially good with tomato or chicken soup.

CHEESE CHOICE

Cheese adds a tangy accent to soups. Worth trying: shredded Swiss cheese on cream of vegetable or tomato rice. Grated Parmesan cheese on mine-strone soup. Shredded sharp yellow cheese sprinkled on jellied consomme. Snippets (shapes cut from thin-sliced cheese) floated on top of soup (good on most kinds).

SOUR CREAM TOPPING

Try a dollop of sour cream atop soup—hot or cold. Good alone or combined with horseradish or watercress. Add parsley or chopped peeled cucumber for chilled cream of celery, chicken, mushroom soup or jellied consomme. Combine sour cream and chives to top beef broth, tomato, jellied consomme, or beef soup.

WHIPPED CREAM GARNISHES

Combine ¼ cup heavy cream (whipped) with ½ teaspoon prepared horseradish; spoon on frozen green pea with ham soup. Or to ¼ cup heavy cream (whipped) add 1 teaspoon grated lime rind, ½ teaspoon sherry (optional) for jellied consomme. Or try ¼ teaspoon minced onion in cream for beef broth-tomato soup.

EASY DUMPLINGS

¼ cup packaged biscuit mix
1 tablespoon milk

Lightly blend biscuit mix and milk. Drop small amounts of dough from tip of a teaspoon into simmering frozen condensed old-fashioned vegetable with beef or condensed vegetable beef soup. Cook for 5 minutes; cover and cook another 5 minutes.

VARIATIONS: 1. Season biscuit mix with 1 teaspoon minced parsley. Add to green pea with ham, clam chowder, or chicken vegetable soup. 2. Add ¼ cup shredded sharp Cheddar cheese to biscuit mix; blend with milk. Add to vegetarian vegetable or tomato soup. 3. Sprinkle dumplings with Parmesan cheese; add to minestrone. 4. Add 1 tablespoon chopped watercress to biscuit mix; cook in turkey noodle soup. 5. Or vary dumplings for turkey noodle by adding 1 teaspoon minced onion.

CURRIED CRAX

⅛ teaspoon curry powder
1 tablespoon butter, melted
½ cup wheat squares or coarsely crumbled saltines

Stir curry powder into butter. Add crackers; heat to brown lightly. Stir often. TIP: Substitute ⅛ teaspoon leaf thyme for curry. Proceed as above. Good on most chicken soups or frozen cream of potato soup.

ONION TIDBITS

¼ teaspoon instant minced onion
1 tablespoon butter, melted
½ cup cheese tidbits

Stir minced onion into butter. Add cheese tidbits; heat to brown lightly. Stir often. Serve on tomato or cream of chicken soup.

SOUP ACCENTS

Almond-Orange: Sprinkle chopped toasted almonds and grated orange rind on heated cream of asparagus or chicken soup.

Diced tomato: Float on jellied consomme or cream of vegetable soup.

Thin sliced onion: Float on top of shimmering jellied consomme.

Chopped celery: Sprinkle on consomme.

Chopped or thinly sliced pickle: Sprinkle on tomato rice soup.

Popcorn: Sprinkle on any soup.

Pretzels: Sprinkle on hearty or thick soups.

CROUTON CREATIONS

Crisp croutons dress up soup easily, can be flavored "to your taste" quickly.

BASIC DIRECTIONS

1 slice white bread, cut into cubes
2 tablespoons butter or margarine, melted

In skillet, brown bread cubes in butter; stir constantly. Season to set off soup flavor.

BASIL OR OREGANO

Sprinkle croutons with ¼ teaspoon sweet basil or ground oregano. Serve with tomato or minestrone soup.

PARMESAN CHEESE

Sprinkle croutons with 1 tablespoon grated Parmesan cheese. Add to frozen old-fashioned vegetable with beef or green pea soup, or minestrone.

CURRY

Sprinkle croutons with curry powder. Add to chicken with rice or cream of chicken or green pea soup.

GARLIC

Melt butter in skillet; add ½ small clove garlic, minced. Lightly mix in bread cubes; cook over low heat, stirring constantly, until bread is crisp and brown. Serve on vegetable or green pea, beef or beef noodle soup.

SAGE OR THYME

Add dash of ground sage or leaf thyme to croutons. Serve with chicken with rice or vegetable soup.

Soup Servers' Almanac

FALL

Brisk winds mark the end of summer. Drive to the country for a pie squash and basket of apples. Pack a vacuum of CLOVE-SEASONED BEEF TOMATO JUG: Combine 1 can each (10½ ounces) condensed beef broth and condensed tomato soup. Stir in 1½ soup cans water, 1 teaspoon lemon juice, dash ground cloves. Simmer a few minutes; pour into vacuum jug and sip (for 4) at a roadside stop.

Leaves changing color in the woods. Follow an autumnal walk with a warming mug of RUSSET SOUP: Combine 1 can (10¼ ounces) frozen condensed old-fashioned vegetable with beef soup, ½ soup can tomato juice, ½ soup can water. Heat and serve to 2 or 3.

Or try ROSY ONION SOUP: 1 can (10½ ounces) condensed onion soup, ½ soup can tomato juice, ½ soup can water. Combine and heat to serve 2 or 3 autumn gardeners.

Early frost. Cover delicate garden plants. Dress children in warm jackets for back-to-school; fix warm lunches, too. HEARTY HAM GUMBO: Brown ¼ cup diced cooked ham in 1 tablespoon butter or margarine. Add 1 can (10½ ounces) condensed chicken gumbo soup, 1 soup can water, dash "Tabasco" sauce. Heat to serve 2 or 3.

Add extra vitamins to lunch for your young scholars. VEGETABLE TURKEY NOODLE: Combine 1 can (10½ ounces) condensed turkey noodle soup, 1 soup can water. Add ¼ cup diced cooked carrots, 1 tablespoon chopped parsley. Heat to make 3 mugs.

Football weather crisp and clear. Pack a blanket and a vacuum bottle of soup. TANGY PEA WITH HAM: Combine 1 can (10½ ounces) frozen condensed green pea with ham soup (thawed), 1 soup can water, generous dash leaf thyme. Heat, stir often, and pour into small vacuum holding 2½ cups; 2 to 3 servings. Double this for extra servings.

CHICKEN RICE CONFETTI is a warmer, too: Combine 1 can (10½ ounces) condensed chicken with rice soup, 1 soup can water, 1 teaspoon finely chopped parsley, 1 teaspoon finely chopped pimiento. Heat; stir often. For 2 or 3.

Late Indian summer with excellent vacation weather. Refresh on arrival with GARDEN TOMATO SOUP: Cook 2 tablespoons chopped green pepper, 2 tablespoons chopped onion, dash oregano in 2 tablespoons butter or margarine until vegetables are tender. Add 1 can (10¾ ounces) condensed tomato rice soup, 1 soup can water. Heat; stir often. Serve to 2 or 3.

Northeasters blowing late October and start of November. Snug time for home parties. Ward off winds outside with warm CHICKEN-ALMOND CURRY SOUP: In saucepan, cook ¼ cup slivered almonds, 2 tablespoons chopped onion, ½ teaspoon curry powder in 1 tablespoon butter or margarine until almonds are lightly browned. Blend in 1 can each (10½ ounces) condensed cream of chicken soup and chicken with rice soup. Add 1½ soup cans water. Heat for 4 to 6 servings.

Sadie Hawkins Day, November 18. Plan a supper soup to please a man. CARAWAY BACON BOWL: Cook 2 ounces Canadian bacon (cut in strips), ¼ cup chopped onion, ¼ teaspoon caraway seed, until onion is tender. Add 1 can (10½ ounces) condensed cream of celery soup, 1 soup can water, 1 cup shredded cabbage. Bring to boil. Cover; simmer 10 minutes or until cabbage is tender. Serve a hearty-eating couple.

For a party, try TRIPLE PLAY SOUPS: Blend 1 can each (10½ ounces) condensed beef noodle, bean with bacon, and cream of celery soup, 2 soup cans water. Add 2 tablespoons chopped parsley, 1 tablespoon Worcestershire; heat and serve to 6 or 8.

Thanksgiving. Begin dinner with a traditional soup . . . onion or cream of mushroom. Or try this unique **GREEN PEPPER CREAM**: In blender, combine 1 can (10½ ounces) condensed cream of celery soup, 1 soup can milk, 3 tablespoons chopped green pepper, and 1 tablespoon chopped onion. Cover; blend until smooth. Pour into saucepan. Heat; stir now and then. 2 to 3 servings. Multiply recipe according to guests you expect.

POST-THANKSGIVING TURKEY SOUP: Cook 1 large chopped onion in 2 tablespoons butter or margarine. Add 1 can (10¾ ounces) condensed cream of vegetable soup and blend with 1½ soup cans water; add 1 can (10½ ounces) condensed turkey noodle soup, 1 cup diced cooked turkey, and 1 tablespoon chopped parsley. Heat; *do not boil*. Stir often and dish up 4 hearty servings.

WINTER

Christmas Eve. Traditional in many homes is an oyster stew supper. Use the frozen soup just as is . . . or garnished with wedges of ripe olive or golden shreds of carrot or cheese. Finish the feast with a fruit bowl (shiny red apples and bright tangerines); Christmas cookies; coffee or tea.

When carolers fill the air with Christmas spirit thank them with **TOMATO SOUP PUNCH**: Combine 1 can (10¾ ounces) condensed tomato soup, 1 soup can milk, ⅛ teaspoon ground cinnamon, dash ground cloves. Beat with a rotary beater. Simmer a few minutes. Garnish each serving with whipped cream. Makes 4 to 5 punch cups.

Sleigh-riding weather frequent between Christmas and New Year's.
Warm winter sports fans with soups that make the most of the last of your
holiday ham. Three ways (count them) to make a little ham go far for
family meals:

1. OYSTER HAM STEW: Combine 1 can (10 ounces) frozen condensed oyster stew with 1 soup can water; heat until partially thawed.
Add 1 cup cubed cooked potatoes, ½ cup diced cooked ham, 1 tablespoon chopped parsley, ⅛ teaspoon leaf thyme. Heat; stir now and then;
do not boil. 3 to 4 servings.

2. HAM CREAM BOWL: Brown ½ cup diced cooked ham in 1 tablespoon butter or margarine. Add 1 can each (10½ ounces) condensed cream
of celery and chicken vegetable soup, 2 soup cans water, 1 tablespoon
chopped parsley, pinch crushed rosemary leaves. Heat; stir often. 4 to 6
servings.

3. HAM FINALE: Combine 1 can (10½ ounces) condensed chicken
noodle soup, 1 soup can water, ¼ cup diced cooked ham, 1 tablespoon
chopped green pepper. Simmer until pepper is tender-crisp; stir. 2 to 3
servings.

Chinese New Year. Between January 21 and February 12, the Chinese
Kitchen God is sent to heaven to report the doings of the household. Be
sure he makes a good report on goings-on at your house.
   Serve an easy CHINESE SOUP: Combine 1 can (10½ ounces) condensed beef broth, 1 soup can water, 2 teaspoons soy sauce. Heat to boiling. Add ¼ cup diced carrots, ¼ cup chopped green beans. Cover; simmer
15 minutes or until vegetables are tender. Serves 2 to 3.

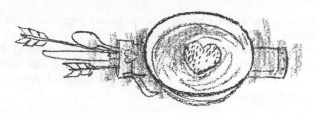

February is long on snow, rain, and holidays. Holiday lunches are easy with MOUNT VERNON GUMBO: Combine 1 can (10½ ounces) condensed chicken gumbo soup, 1 soup can water, ¼ cup cooked crab, fish, or shrimp. Heat; stir now and then. 2 to 3 servings.

VALENTINE CROUTON SOUP: Drain and cook 1 can (2 ounces) mushroom stems and pieces with 1 tablespoon chopped parsley in 1 tablespoon butter or margarine until mushrooms are lightly browned. Add 1 can (10½ ounces) condensed chicken noodle soup, 1 soup can water, 1 tablespoon sherry (optional). Heat; stir. Cut small hearts out of bread slices, brown lightly in butter. Top each serving with a heart crouton. Serve to your love and you.

Or simply serve the heart croutons on rosy red Tomato Soup.

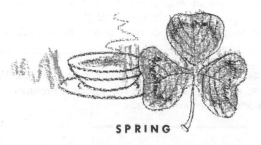

SPRING

March windy and sunny. Time to order seeds. St. Patrick's Day and green is on the menu. For a simple celebration, just heat a can of cream of potato soup as directed. Garnish with parsley or watercress. Or you might serve green pea soup . . . topped with a fluff of unsweetened whipped cream.

SPRING GREEN SOUP tastes like a party: Cook ¼ cup chopped onion in 1 tablespoon butter or margarine until tender. Stir in 1 can (10½ ounces) condensed cream of celery soup, 1½ soup cans milk, ½ cup drained chopped cooked spinach, dash sweet basil. Heat; stir often. 3 servings.

April showers and Lenten meals call for hearty meatless soups. A quartet of chowders.

GARDEN CHOWDER: Combine 1 can (10¼ ounces) frozen condensed clam chowder (New England style), 1 soup can water, ½ cup cooked carrots (cut in strips), 2 tablespoons chopped parsley. Heat; stir often; *do not boil*. 2 to 3 servings.

SHRIMP CHOWDER: Cook ¼ cup chopped onion in 2 tablespoons butter or margarine until tender. Blend in 2 cans (10½ ounces each) condensed cream of celery or mushroom soup, 1 soup can each of milk and water, 1 cup cooked shrimp (6-ounce can, drained), 2 tablespoons chopped parsley, dash pepper. Heat. Garnish each serving with paprika. 6 to 8 servings. TUNA CHOWDER: Repeat the previous recipe, except omit the shrimp and add 1 cup drained flaked tuna (7-ounce can) instead. LOBSTER OR CRAB CHOWDER: You can make the same soup with 1 cup flaked cooked lobster or crab (or 6½-ounce can, drained) instead of shrimp or tuna.

For an elegant Lenten soup serve SOUP THYME: Blend 1 can (10¾ ounces) condensed cream of vegetable soup with 1 soup can water and ¼ teaspoon ground thyme. Heat; stir now and then. Garnish each serving with unsweetened whipped cream or sour cream. Serve to 2 or 3.

Easter Sunday dinner is a family tradition in many homes. Whether the main course is ham or lamb, plan a soup for a perfect prelude . . . perhaps chicken with rice or cream of asparagus.

Mother's Day and time to flatter the daily soup maker with a flavorful bowl pretty as a bouquet. MINTED PEA SOUP: Blend 1 can (11¼ ounces) condensed green pea soup and 1 soup can water. Add ¼ cup thinly sliced carrot, 1 tablespoon sliced green onion, and 1 teaspoon crushed dried mint flakes. Heat; stir now and then. Garnish with sour cream for 2 or 3 servings.

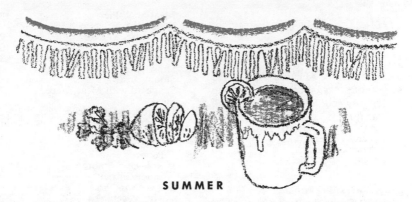

SUMMER

Early warm days relieved by cool soups to sip. TOMATO TANG: Blend 1 can (10½ ounces) condensed tomato soup and 1 soup can water. Stir in ½ teaspoon grated lemon rind. Place in refrigerator for at least 4 hours. Serve in chilled bowls; garnish with parsley or lemon slice to refresh 2 or 3.

Beware sudden chill after early-summer swim. Warm up with CONSOMME RISOTTO: Combine 1 can (10½ ounces) condensed consomme, 1 soup can water, and ¼ cup cooked rice. Heat; stir often. Serve to 2 or 3.

One hot dish is the old rule for a cold meal. Make yours SAVORY CONSOMME: Cook ¼ cup chopped green pepper and 1 tablespoon thinly sliced green onion in 2 tablespoons butter or margarine until tender. Add 2 cans (10½ ounces each) condensed consomme, 1½ soup cans water, and 2 whole cloves. Simmer a few minutes to blend flavors. Remove cloves before serving to 4 or 5.

August sunny; corn ripens. Try kernels in CORN OYSTER STEW: Cook 2 tablespoons small thin green pepper strips and 2 tablespoons chopped green onion in 1 tablespoon butter or margarine until vegetables are tender. Add 1 can (10 ounces) frozen condensed oyster stew, 1 soup can water, and ½ cup cooked whole kernel corn. Heat until soup is thawed; stir now and then. 2 to 3 servings.

For small-fry sailors, deck a green pea "sea" of soup with a cracker SAILBOAT: Spread 2 round crackers with peanut butter. Cut 1 saltine in half diagonally so you have two triangles. Stand the half cracker in the peanut butter to make a "sail". Float sailboat on soup. 2 sailboats for *fair weather ahead.*

Index

(*Continued*)

(Continued)

194

(Continued)

(*Continued*)

(Continued)

198

"To make the best,
begin with the best—
then cook with extra care."